Imperialism in East Africa

D. Wadada Nabudere

Imperialism in East Africa

Volume 1: Imperialism and Exploitation

D. Wadada Nabudere

Zed Press, 57 Caledonian Road, London N1 9DN

Imperialism in East Africa, Vol. I: *Imperialism and Exploitation* was first published by Zed Press, 57 Caledonian Road, London N1 9DN in 1981.

Copyright © D. Wadada Nabudere, 1981

Copyedited by Beverley Brown
Proofread by Penelope Fryxell
Designed by Mayblin/Shaw
Cover Design by Jan Brown
Typeset by Donald Typesetting
Printed by Redwood Burn, Trowbridge, Wiltshire.

British Library Cataloguing in Publication Data
Nabudere, D. Wadada
Imperialism in East Africa
Vol. I: Imperialism and exploitation
1. Africa, East — History
I. Title
976.6   DT365
ISBN 0 905762 99 1

U.S. Distributor
Lawrence Hill and Co., 520 Riverside Avenue, Westport, Conn. 06880, U.S.A.

Dedication

Dedicated to those who made their contribution to
the first struggles against imperialist penetration
— and in particular to **Machemba** (Tanzania),
Kabarega (Uganda) and **Mekatilili** (Kenya).

Contents

Tables

Preface

The integration and exploitation of East Africa by British and German imperialists is deeply rooted in the capitalist development of Europe. Fore-runners of monopoly capitalist colonization such as the slave trade and 'outpost colonization' only prepared the ground for a more permanently based exploitation under capitalist imperialism.

This later imperialism brought new forms of exploitation based on an entirely new mode of production within East Africa itself. The theoretical basis for this exploitation is articulated in the subsequent volume, *Imperialism and Integration* (forthcoming). Here it is enough to note that the new imperialism uprooted indigenous structures of East Africa and imposed an entirely alien structure which was both exploitative and oppressive. In the course of the development of imperialist relations, the people's resistance strengthened until it was overthrown. This overturn of colonialism did not, however, eliminate the exploitative relations, which continued under multilateral imperialism.

Under neo-colonialism the economies of East Africa continued to serve the interests of the monopolies of the imperialist countries and the people's consciousness was reawakened to exploitation in its new forms.

The struggle of the people of East Africa continues, but such a struggle can only succeed if led by the working class in the new democratic revolution which alone can bring down the power of imperialism in East Africa.

The present volume is a short resume of the political economy of each of the three countries of East Africa. It is written as an introduction to a proper understanding of the issues of regional integration under imperialism, which will be dealt with in Volume Two.

D. Wadada Nabudere
Dar es Salaam

1

Part One
Colonial Exploitation and Revolt

1. The Scramble and Integration

Early Linkages

Imperialist contacts between Europe and East Africa must be dated from the Portuguese voyages of 'discovery'. But these expeditions were preceded by even earlier contacts between Europe and the East African or 'Ausanitic' Coast. Recent historical researches have unearthed references as far back as the first century A.D. that suggest trade links between the East Coast and Southern Arabia.[1] That this early Arabian trade also reached Europe is indicated by the Greek text, *Voyage Around the Erythrean Sea*. Among the goods exchanged for Arabian iron implements by the peoples of the East African Coast were ivory, palm oil, rhinoceros horn, tortoise shell, cinnamon, frankincense and slaves.

This form of trade with Arabia, China and India continued right up to the period when direct European entry signalled a new era in the history not only of East Africa but also of its trading partners. All of them came under the sway of the forces that were at work in Europe — the very forces that were increasingly pushing Europe into newer pastures.[2] This push from Europe took place sporadically over a long period, spearheaded by a succession of nations as each came to prominence. The objectives of the colonizing powers were broadly similar but by no means identical, and the whole movement can only be understood in its aims and consequences when it is examined concretely and scientifically, exposing the real internal dynamic that propelled it forward.

Although the time-scale, participants, and immediate aims differed, this expansionism, particularly in the 18th and 19th Centuries, had one common objective: the accumulation of surplus products (including 'surplus' human products known as slaves) as well as surplus value created in these countries. The distinction between surplus products and surplus value will be important, because it allows us to distinguish the different phases of development of the productive forces and social relations in Europe, which unleashed new forces of imperialist expansionism and domination. Our starting point, therefore, in considering the impact of imperialism in its different phases on East African societies, is to differentiate and study the internal dynamics of the European societies responsible for this impact.

It is in this context that the earliest Portuguese contacts in the region can be characterized as mercantilist imperialist — that is, concerned with surplus products — for their main objective in East Africa was to 'seize the whole trade of the Indian Ocean and of the distant Spice Islands'[3] from rival traders, and to establish points of supply for their vessels along their plundering routes. Thus, although their original push outwards, from the attack on Ceuta in 1415, was mainly a crusade against Islam in North-west and West Africa, it was the attraction of large commercial profits further south, from gold dust, ivory and slaves, that led the Portuguese on to the Cape of Good Hope and thence to the East Coast of Africa, in an outward expansion concerned with breaking the Venetian monopoly of the old overland trade routes via Asia Minor.[4]

This kind of expansion did not require the establishment of colonial settlements. In any case, the low level of technological development in Europe at the time, all production being based on unmechanized serf labour, limited material resources to an extent which would have precluded overseas settlement.[5] Moreover, the prevailing physical conditions did not permit large new settlements. Mercantilist imperialism was therefore based on *trade*. The imperialist power merely set up a plundering outpost from where it collected its exotic products from the people either through merchants' local agents or even as tribute from local rulers — in the port of Kilwa in 1502 Vasco da Gama on his second voyage forced Ibrahim, the ruler of the port, to ransom himself for a tribute of 1,500 gold meticals and to recognize the supremacy of the King of Portugal over his territory.[6]

By 1509 the Portuguese had established domination over the whole East African Coast,[7] giving them access to all the products of the region, including slaves. They exported much of this wealth to India, in exchange for Indian textiles for the home market. The Portuguese garrison at Fort Jesus, Mombasa, became a permanent outpost for Portuguese trade for over a century and a half.

Portugal's long hegemony over the East Coast was finally challenged, not by a more powerful imperialist power but by the force of a small Arab emirate. In 1692 a raiding party from Oman destroyed the Portuguese settlements at Zanzibar and Pate, and finally, in 1696, Oman's siege of Fort Jesus ended nearly two centuries of Portuguese presence on the East Coast north of the Ruvuma River, though sporadic scuffles went on until the 1740s. Despite this victory for the Arabs, internal dissension among the Oman's followers, including the struggles by the Mazarai, led by Atman Mazrui, to establish an autonomous enclave at Mombasa and Pemba, weakened Oman's grip on the coast, so that it was not until the French showed their interest in the area that British imperialists moved in to attempt an alliance with Seyyid Said of Oman. This occurred after 1806, and the events that then took place in the area were greatly influenced by the developments in the British economy.

In Britain the Industrial Revolution had transformed the basis of the mode of production from home-based serf labour to a 'free' labour force no longer bound to the soil or to feudal masters. This new capitalist mode of production implied a shift in the conception of trade and a new inward-looking concentration on the development of production which necessarily affected attitudes towards overseas territories. In contrast with earlier forms of colonialism — first the 'Empire of Outposts'[8] (1598–1763) and then the policy of 'internal expansion',[9] as evident in the colonization of Quebec (ending around 1870) — Britain was now embarked on a third period, that of colonialist imperialism, or 'free trade imperialism'.[10]

This phase of British imperialism was in fact the second wave of European expansion in East Africa. The previous period had involved rivalries between the European powers, especially Britain and France, which had had its own bourgeois revolution in 1793 but was less economically developed than Britain. France's imperialist ambitions had been increasingly challenged by Britain which had emerged as the undisputed great power in Africa, Asia and America, after the Congress of Vienna in 1815 marked the end of the Napoleonic wars.[11] Britain's challenge to French expansionism in Africa meant that France was eventually forced to abandon its triangular trade based on French brandy and firearms, Indian goods and, most profitably, African slaves. Already by the end of the 18th Century, France's slave trade had risen appreciably, and, oblivious to the humanist sentiments of the French Revolution, it continued almost unabated despite British efforts to eliminate it in this area, as part of its efforts to prepare the ground for 'legitimate trade'. The Ile de France in the Indian Ocean just off the East African Coast was the centre of the slave trade, which had been legalized there by Napoleon in 1802. This island became a point of contestation between the two imperialist powers and consequently Britain was in 1798 forced to strike an alliance with the Oman in the form of a treaty under which the Oman agreed to stop trading with France and Holland. As a British colonial historian has stated: 'It was, too, to maintain the friendly relations so established with this strategically placed sultanate that the British were a little tardy in launching their anti-slave trade campaign in the western half of the Indian Ocean'.[12] With the assistance of the Oman, the British were able to capture the French possession in 1810 and rename it Mauritius. On the basis of the Moresby Treaty the struggle against France and the slave trade continued, leading to France's total loss of this trade and of other territories to Britain.[13] Thus Britain's campaign against the slave trade can be seen to be very much subject to strategic advantages that offered themselves.

Free Trade and Philanthropy

French rivalry once subdued, British imperialism turned to other matters and eventually to the question of consolidating its own territories in the area. Given Britain's total power in the Indian Ocean, Arab trade and colonial enclaves played only a subsidiary role. Eventually robbed of its material base, the slave trade gradually slackened, but in the 1820s Britain was not yet ready to establish itself fully on the East African Coast in order to implant a new imperialism. British missionaries, following on the heels of the slavers, were but an advance guard, much as the Portuguese had been, preparing the way, softening and making malleable Africa's response for the approaching wave of European expansion.

British attitudes towards the slave trade between 1790 and 1860 were to involve a critical balance of ideological, political and economic forces in which the whole conception of colonialism was to be rethought. The industrial bourgeoisie, which was consolidating its class power over the British state, was not in favour of establishing new colonies. As early as the 1790s and even before, its ideologies called on Britain to 'emancipate the colonies',[14] thereby earning themselves the title of 'Little Englanders'.[15] Liberals and Conservatives alike advocated the withdrawal of British troops from the colonies — an understandable position, given the new climate of free trade and its emphasis on home production, where state restrictions and the burdensome expenses of war could be met only by higher taxation. Disraeli, the Conservative leader, declared: 'The colonies will be independent in a few years, and they are a millstone on our necks.'[16] The new industrial bourgeoisie, keen to invest its savings in means of expanding production, was therefore averse to colonization, while the colonists, themselves under the slogan 'no payment of taxes without representation', equally demanded the 'freeing' of the colonies. Also, it should not be forgotten that those colonies which were being set free in the late 18th and early 19th Centuries were, as Knowles reminds us, colonies of 'racial expansion', inhabited by the white races.[17]

It was because of the lack of interest in colonization in the early 19th Century that a British protectorate over Mombasa, offered by the local Arab sultan in 1824 to a certain Captain Owen, was so short-lived: Britain was not yet ready for a new colonization drive and Captain Owen was forced to withdraw his representatives by 1826.[18] The British-assisted restoration of Seyyid Said's overlordship in the area, and the resultant shift of his capital from Oman to Zanzibar in 1840, was a smokescreen behind which British imperialism put into effect its old policy of rivalry with France and later Germany in the Indian Ocean, first through the India Office and later by direct consular representation in Zanzibar. This line of policy was adequate to protect its interests at this time.

From the 1840s onwards it became Britain's policy to eliminate the slave trade, and later slavery itself, as the precondition of its free trade capitalism. As already indicated, this new form of production emphasized capitalist production at home and free trade overseas, not only with other sovereign countries but also with the colonies. According to this doctrine, countries which had a comparative advantage in the production of particular goods could exchange them in a free market with others which had a similar advantage in other goods, and in this way the wealth of all civilized nations, 'by one common tie of interest and intercourse',[19] would grow to unequalled heights. This progressive outlook of the young British industrial bourgeoisie, reflecting the new mode of production and the new morality, depended upon the existence of suitable trading goods in other countries, and hence the creation of new forms of production.

As far as colonies were concerned, this production would be of agricultural goods to be bought by British industries. Thus, the logic of free trade would eventually require a certain minimum level of production initiated in the colonies themselves. Clearly, if East Africa were to raise its level of agricultural production to meet the import needs of a British economy geared towards industrial growth at home and free trade abroad, a stable domestic economy was required. The slave trade which had ravaged the region for centuries would have to be stopped. To the extent that early British capitalism succeeded in introducing new productive power in East Africa, it was progressive, even revolutionary. But although the anti-slavery campaign did succeed in the end, its policy of introducing 'legitimate trade' to the interior of East Africa did not provide a simple answer to the problem of the slave trade, since the region relied, up to the 1880s, on slave labour to produce and, to some extent, to sell its own products. Furthermore, by the time all forms of slave trade and slavery had been brought to a halt, the young and revolutionary English capitalism which had demanded its demise had itself been transmuted into monopoly capitalism. The potentially revolutionary effects of anti-slave trade capitalism on East African production could not be seen through, and the effort turned out to be no more than a prelude to integrating the region into a decadent and parasitic monopoly capitalism. However, this is to anticipate. We must first trace the history of the relation between free trade and the slave trade in the region up to 1880.

British policy in this free trade period was aimed at the containment of other imperialist powers such as France. This was necessary if British efforts to prepare the area for integration with its own production were to succeed. Although able to get rid of French imperialism and its 'illegitimate' trade in slaves, Britain was soon faced by a new rival in East Africa, this time in the field of 'legitimate trade'. This newcomer was the United States, which by 1808 had appeared in the area with attractive textile merchandise known as *merikani*. As a colony of Britain itself, the U.S. had been excluded from the Indian Ocean trade by the monopoly given to the East India Company in 1600. But after Independence in 1776, it had begun to develop its own textile industry and was now able to engage in world trade. In September 1833 it signed a commercial treaty with Zanzibar, entitling American citizens to trade in all Zanzibari ports on payment of a 5% duty; the United States Government was also allowed to establish a consulate in Zanzibar. But Britain was close behind, and in 1839 had also signed a commercial treaty with Zanzibar. Its main purpose was supposedly to consolidate existing diplomatic relations, but it also, under Article 10 of the treaty, prohibited the granting of any 'monopoly or exclusive privilege of sale' within the Sultan's dominions except in ivory and gum-copal on the East Coast. The treaty otherwise insisted on a free trade policy. France too, now interested in free trade but still with an eye on slave trade, signed a commercial treaty with Zanzibar in 1847. The Germans followed with their own treaty in the same year.

As well as establishing close relations with the Sultan in Zanzibar, where a consulate-general had been established in 1841, Britain benefited commercially from the presence of a large subject merchant class which, although also trading in the goods of its rivals, favoured the handling of British goods from India and England. As Ingham has commented: 'The *banyans* at that time handled the greater part of Zanzibar's trade and Britain benefited indirectly in that, with the exception of the *merikani* cloth imported from the United States, most goods brought to East Africa by traders of all nations were made in Britain.'[20] Thus British hegemony as the 'Workshop of the World' was now assured in the area.

But characteristic of this period was the fact that neither Britain (still with a larger interest to mind in India), the Americans, the French, nor even the Germans, had any intentions of establishing *political* control over the region. This stance had an economic and material basis in the preoccupation of these countries with their own industrial development, development which would itself yield the material conditions for the subsequent phase of political scramble and integration.

But before this could happen the problem of slavery had to be finally dealt with. By the second quarter of the 19th Century Arab caravans had begun to penetrate the interior in search of slaves, carrying 'legitimate' goods for which the 'illegitimate' slave goods were exchanged. The whole of the coastal hinterland was depopulated as a result of this 'legitimate/illegitimate' trade. '*Banyans* who had lived in Zanzibar for many years told Colonel Rigby, Political Agent and Consul there from 1858 and 1861, that when they first came to the coast the whole country behind Kilwa was densely populated. In Rigby's time it was necessary to travel into the interior for eighteen days before coming upon a village.'[21]

When David Livingstone arrived in the vicinity of Lake Nyasa he noted that local districts which in 1859 had been flourishing agricultural communities, some two or three years later contained 'not a single human for distances of as much as a hundred miles'.[24] In fact, 'free', 'legitimate' trade was thriving on the slave trade: true, Arab traders had turned their attention mainly to ivory after the British embargo on the slave trade in Zanzibar, yet by using slaves to carry ivory to the coast alongside the caravans, they availed themselves of a valuable commodity which, unlike other modes of transport, could itself be sold on arrival at the coast for a handsome price. Slaves thus played a dual role in the transaction — as transporters and as commodities in the market-place.[25]

The growth in the slave trade continued despite British attempts at prohibition. In 1807 the British Parliament had outlawed the trade, with very little practical result. Moreover, the 1833 Act which abolished slavery did not apply to British 'overseas territories', only to the 'colonies'. India, a vital link in the trade of both slaves and 'legitimate goods', was exempted from the 1833 Act, along with Ceylon and Saint Helena. Zanzibar was not a British colony and hence measures affecting slaves could be negotiated only by treaty. Since domestic slavery was well entrenched there, the British Government was reluctant to enforce abolition too stringently for fear of endangering its relations with the Sultan. Only after the British presence in the area was consolidated did Britain pursue a firm policy against slavery.

In 1859 Zanzibar's import-export trade was valued at £1,664,598. By 1879 it had increased to £2,200,000. Nearly three-sevenths of the imports consisted of cotton goods, of which U.S. *merikani* cloth topped the list with goods to the value of £95,000. British goods took second place with £67,000 and British India was close behind also with £67,000.[24] Thus British goods were clearly in the lead (since Indian goods were effectively British goods). Other goods included rice, guns, and gunpowder imported by Belgium, Britain and Germany. The main exports were ivory, cloves, and a new product from Kilwa district called Indian rubber. There was also some millet, hides and skins, copra, sesamum, gum copal and ochilla.

However, by 1879 Germany was quickly catching up with British trade, a fact that was to be significant in the scramble for this area between Britain and Germany in the next phase of rivalry. By 1874 German imports had risen to £168,000, pushing the U.S. out of second position, with France falling behind the rest. This so impressed the Germans that they came to believe their trade was greater than that of the British [25] — a belief that was perhaps to determine their aggressive approach in the scramble. In fact, the extent of Britain's lead should be estimated with reference to goods in transit, including the Indian trade. For instance, in 1879 imports from India to Zanzibar were valued at £252,000 and exports to India at £176,000, and of this 'more than half of the Indian imports were in fact only Indian "in transit" [having] come from Britain via Bombay'.[26] A similar proportion of the exports destined for India were in fact for Britain. 'Thus British business actually accounted for at least one-third of the imports and more than half of the exports.'[27] In addition some of the goods handled by Indian merchants on behalf of Germany and France were also British; although this share must have decreased by 1879, it should be taken into account in indicating the hegemony of British trade at the end of this phase of integration.

British integrative activities in this period also included the establishment of communication links. Apart from the shipping necessary for trading, British enterprise established a mail service, provided by the British India Company in 1872 between Aden and Zanzibar. It also contracted with the French to link this service to the Comoro Islands and Majunga. The same service was linked to Europe and India by Mackinnon's British India Steamship Company and later by the British India Company. A provisional post office could thus be established, as indeed it was in 1878 at Zanzibar and later on a permanent footing. In 1877 an application by the Eastern Telegraph Company to lay a cable from Aden to Natal was made and granted; cable-laying began in 1879. Britain was well poised to claim the area.

The Missionary Movement and the Anti-Slavery Campaign
One of the main agencies for spreading the anti-slavery campaign and

disseminating the ideology of free 'legitimate' trade was the missionaries. In a letter to Professor Sidgwick of Cambridge in 1858, David Livingstone had revealed this 'secret', declaring: 'I believe the highlands are healthy — the wild vine flourishes there. Europeans with a speedy transport to the coast would collect and transit the produce to the sea and in the course of time, say when my head is low, free labour on the African soil might render slave labour which is notoriously dear labour quite unprofitable.'[28]

In many cases merchant and missionary activities were co-ordinated. In 1878 a band of Scottish merchants interested in missionary work launched a steamer on Lake Nyasa to interfere with the slave trade and offer instead facilities for legitimate trade. It was hoped that this would encourage the production of coffee and tobacco as alternative commodities. Knowles commented: 'They did so successfully that they added a new region to the British Empire and Nyasaland became a protectorate in 1890.'[29] Johnston pinpoints the role of the missionary in colonization for private profit:

> The value of missionaries as pioneers of civilization, which this country seems impelled to extend . . . cannot be overestimated. These pioneers do not stop to ask whether it will pay to venture their lives and their funds in these remote countries . . . . They make all the experiments and others reap the profit. On the results of their researches commerce is able to decide its timid steps and eventually we possess sufficient data on which to determine whether it is right and necessary for the Government to seal with its intervention the work which these missionaries began.[30]

Indeed this pioneering work was the great service that missionaries offered to British free-trade imperialism in this period — in East Africa they were the first Europeans to establish themselves on the mainland.[31] The first of the missionaries, Ludwig Krapf of the British Church Missionary Society, arrived in Zanzibar in January 1844 after a brief stop-over at Mombasa, where he returned to settle in the same year. Learning the Kiswahili language, within four years he was able to translate the New Testament into Kiswahili and to compile an outline grammar of it.[32] Krapf was soon joined by Rev. J. Rebmann. In 1846 they set up a station at Rabai, and from there made regular exploratory visits to the interior, as far afield as Kilimanjaro, Kitui and Usambara. They were joined by a third recruit, J. Erhardt. It was on the basis of a rough map, drawn by Erhardt and published in London in 1856, that their somewhat limited and sketchy expeditions into the deep interior could be followed through more scientifically by professional explorers such as Burton and Speke in 1857, and later Stanley.

It was the activities of these later explorers that gave the imperialists of Europe a more definite view of the interior, and cleared the ground for the entry of finance capital. With the transformation of capitalism into its monopoly phase, the scramble for the partition of Africa began. The arrival of Livingstone added further impetus to exploration; with the zeal of a free trader he set up missions and centres of Christianity, which were to exist 'side by side with instruction in agriculture and with encouragement in trade'.[33] By the 1880s the stage was set for the scramble; in the words of Coupland,

> Golden expectations of the wealth to be won somewhere in the teeming heart of Africa had been conjured up by reports of the first explorers; and the interest taken in the second phase of exploration, which opened in 1874, was quite as much commercial interest as scientific, philanthropic or political. A little more light, and Africa might be found possessing more riches than the East.[34]

The Scramble Begins

In the period following 1870 'the Empire, and not merely Great Britain, became a world power', as it attained 'coherence . . . [and] world unity'.[35] A period of 'constructive imperialism' had begun:

> Imperial conferences became possible as never before. Colonial exhibitions were arranged, a rapid investment of British capital in the colonies took place, emigration was stimulated when it was no longer exile from civilization. The world shrank; an imperial policy became workable. *Laissez-faire* was abandoned both with regard to the tropical and the self-governing dominions. The world economics of free trade began to give way to imperial economics.[36]

This transformation of imperialist relations both reflected and was dependent upon the monopoly capitalism which in this phase came increasingly to dominate economic relations in Europe and in the United States. Capital was centralized and concentrated, small enterprises being swallowed up by larger ones. Dominant sectors of the economy came under the control of monopoly banks and industries. In pursuit of higher rates of profit from the production of raw materials and food, the big bourgeoisie now controlling these huge banks and industries increasingly competed for markets and outlets for the export of capital, under constant pressure from other monopolies pursuing the same goals in other imperialist countries. The formation of cartels, combinations, syndicates, trusts and other forms of monopoly in each of the imperialist countries became the determinant form of international relations. On the basis of these monopolies, a division of the world was carried out.

In the developed form of monopoly capitalism, as distinct from its predecessor, competitive capitalism, five main characteristics became evident:

1) Concentration of production and capital intensified into the creation of monopolies, playing a decisive role in economic life;

2) The merger of bank capital and industrial capital into 'finance capital'

13

created a financial oligarchy as a distinct class, international in its interests, which lived by 'clipping coupons';

3) The export of capital acquired paramount importance, although the export of goods as such continued;

4) International capitalist associations were formed by competing monopoly bourgeoisies, on the basis of which they shared the world among themselves;

5) The territorial division of the world, which began afresh in the 1880s under the control of the largest capitalist powers, was completed, so that in the future only *re-division* on the basis of agreement or war was possible.[39]

These features marked modern imperialism as the highest stage of capitalism, a stage in which the possession of colonies became the only basis of survival by the monopolies of each imperialist country, with the result that all productive activity in the newly acquired colonies, as well as in those already held, would be tailored to the interests of the imperialist powers, thus stunting any indigenous development. The colonized countries were integrated with the imperialist countries, not only in a new economic form, but also politically.

Competition for Colonial Markets

The new forces that shook East Africa in this period arose from these new developments in the economies of Europe, the United States and — somewhat later — Japan. For a time Britain kept up the illusion of free trade. New competitors, however, were on the horizons ready to challenge not only British home markets but also the colonial markets. We have seen that this challenge was already incipient in the activities of Germany. Before 1884 Germany had shown little interest in colonization, although various scholars and activists were advocating it. Interest caught on, however, when Carl Peters founded the Society for German Colonization. In 1885 the Society was incorporated as the German East Africa Company, to which were ceded all 'treaties' which Peters had been busy signing with the chiefs in this part of Africa. The company had huge monopolies as its shareholders. Two monopolists (the banker Karl von der Heydt and the industrialist Friedrich Krupp), the official Overseas Trading Corporation and a few other capitalists took control of the company and therefore of the colonization process which Carl Peters was carrying out. Bismarck, who in 1881 had declared, 'As long as I am Chancellor, we will carry on no colonial policies', was now ready to give full support to German colonization. By 1884 the 'national impulse' compelled him to engage in imperialist division and colonization. Although Germany had been a late starter in its industrialization, by the 1860s it was already catching up in many sectors of the economy with Britain and the U.S., partly due to the cartel system. These cartels, or joint bodies representing a number of enterprises, were able to fix prices, sales, production and output policies. German industry benefited to the extent that capital could be concentrated more quickly by avoiding waste and making competition in the home market more disciplined. By 1875 German banks and industry were 'indissolubly linked together' in such a manner that the banks directed industrial policy. Indeed, it was the banks that encouraged the formation of cartels in the industries they financed, in order to minimize competition.[38] By 1884 these developments compelled Germany to engage in the scramble for East Africa.

In October 1885 Bismarck called an international conference in Berlin to agree on the policies of partition with the other big imperialist powers, 'in order that the new occupations on the coasts of the African Continent may be held to be effective'.[39] Two treaties between Germany and Britain sealed the division in East Africa. The first, signed on 14 June 1890, partitioned the territories on the mainland over which the Sultan of Zanzibar had some claim. These, despite protests by the Sultan, were now taken by Germany with British consent. The second, signed on 1 July 1890, settled Anglo-German spheres of influence by giving Germany the southern part of the region along a line south of Lake Victoria, and Britain the northern part around the Upper Nile, establishing a British protectorate over Zanzibar and Pemba. In exchange for the rights of the Sultan over her claims over the mainland and over Heligoland, Britain finalized the partition of East Africa with Germany. Although some compensation was paid to the Sultan, it was insignificant compared to the privileges the Germans received.[40] Having obtained partition, Germany moved to integrate the area in three stages: first, by sending punitive expeditions into the interior against 'recalcitrant chiefs'; second, by setting up military posts on caravan routes, at the centres of maritime trade, at places where European merchants and missionaries had settled, and at the headquarters of agents of the Sultan of Zanzibar or local chiefs; and third, by establishing a civilian colonial regime to replace the initial military regime led by Wissman.[41] Any resistance from the African people in the interior was crushed. That the African people did make efforts to repulse this external aggression has been documented by Charles Dundas as part of the British Government's attempt to demonstrate Germany's unfitness to govern.[42] By these various means the ground was laid for subsequent economic integration.

'Strategic' or Economic Interests?
British colonization took more or less the same pattern wherever it appeared, ranging from India to Egypt, without the need for an aggressive profile. Its partitioning activities were extensive, in proportion with its position of world hegemony. Thus it appeared as if its concern for the suppression of the slave trade was strategically rather than economically motivated;[43] and the activities of the British Imperial East Africa Company have often been interpreted in this light. Such an explanation, however, is inadequate; the argument that Britain was at that time less interested in acquiring new territories than in defending its existing possessions — in particular the strategic route through the Suez Canal to India — does not prove that it had no imperialist ambitions. More importantly, Britain's concern to smash the slave trade, as a threat to its own free trade policy, is evidence that it was

motivated by imperialist ambitions. By the 1880s any possibilities of 'free trade' were illusory — so illusory that when Britain awoke to the reality of the scramble it pursued its own colonization with such zeal and violence that its earlier pretensions to philanthropy could now fool only those with a merely superficial understanding of the period's historical movements. Only a materialist world outlook reveals this movement correctly, and it is this outlook that 'official science', as Lenin called it, tried 'by a conspiracy of silence to kill'.[44] But the facts are intractable, and Britain soon unmasked her intentions in East Africa. With the appointment of a Commissioner to preside over the protectorate that had been declared over Uganda, she now, according to Ingham, 'accepted her responsibility': 'Thrusting behind her anti-imperialist outlook which had dominated her nineteenth-century policy Britain now began a process of annexation of Uganda, wherever possible making use of agreements but employing force where necessary.'[45]

This 'responsibility' was extended to other areas. A protectorate was also declared over what was then called British East Africa, to put the official seal on the activities of the British Imperial East African Company, which since 1885 had been granted a charter by the British Government to acquire territory from 'native chiefs' in the British sphere of influence, by treaty, purchase 'or otherwise', to establish civil and judicial administration of the territory under the company's rule and to undertake trading operations, as well as taking over concessions from the Sultan.

For purposes of integration into a free trade area, East Africa found itself included in the area later to be known as the Congo Basin Treaty area, mainly created by the rivalry between Belgium, Portugal, France and Germany. This involved East Africa in a tangle of diplomatic relations. King Leopold of the Belgians, 'enthused' with the idea of creating an international association for the opening up of Africa to Europe, found himself caught up in various claims and counterclaims. Without any definite claims to the area, Britain was nonetheless opposed to any other powers being installed there, and struck up an alliance with Portugal, an old imperialist power with long-standing claims to the Congo area and neighbouring territories. But Portugal, while using British support against France and Germany, also secretly worked against the British in alliance with the French.[46] The result was an international conference attended by 13 nations which tried to counter-balance the conflicting interests in the area. The conference discussed freedom of trade in the Congo Basin and Estuary, freedom of navigation on the Congo and the Niger, and formalities to be observed in connection with the occupation of new territories on the African coast. The final agreements signed in Berlin in 1885 and Brussels in 1890 were later revised after the First World War by the victors, at Saint Germain-en-Laye in 1919. Within the Basin it was agreed to abolish the slave trade and to bar preferential tariffs, only allowing up to 10% duty for revenue purposes to the governing power. Free navigation on the Congo and the Niger was assured to all parties, as was the principle of equality between the signatories over the resources by settlement or industrial development. Finally, the zone was declared neutral in case of war. In 1919 the limitation of customs duty imposed earlier was removed, allowing duty of up to 20% for revenue purposes. Under the mandate over Tanganyika after the First World War these requirements were still applied to that territory.

It is notable that, despite the multilateral character of these arrangements for the exploitation of the area, the bilateral relationship between each imperialist power and its individual colonies inevitably became the dominant relation in the region, since, despite the 'open door' policy, no international machinery existed to supervise the system, as was to be the case in the period of multilateral imperialism after the Second World War. Moreover, monopoly capitalism was not adequately developed to multilateralise itself. In this period, the era of bilateral imperialism, Leopold's internationalist coloniz-ation was soon superseded by the 'nationalization' of the Congo Free State in 1908, when the Belgian Government took over the territory and administered it as its own colony. Imperialist state monopolies were soon running many enterprises, with the result that 'free trade' was merely a cover for an other-wise monopolistic situation in which the various European states operating in the Basin were using different mechanisms to integrate their respective colonies into their own economies.

A clear example of this was the *Oscar Chinn* case, in which a British navigation firm was discriminated against by Belgian freight rate policy, giving a virtual monopoly advantage to a Belgian company in the so-called free trade zone.[47] A ruling by the Permanent Court of Justice against Oscar Chinn confirmed that no 'existing vested interests' were infringed by the monopoly to UNITRA, the Belgian firm. In the same period British policies in the three territories of East Africa also went far towards consolidating British monopoly interests against the other signatories, thus giving Britain increasing advantage over its competitors. As Brett argues:

> During the twenties British manufacturers and merchants were happy enough with this situation because they were still able to compete successfully in the area and the reciprocal privileges accorded them in the rest of the zone offset the effects of competition in the British territories. Their position inside the latter was also reinforced by advantages of language and contacts, not to mention the Government's commitments to buy British, which was effectively realized through the work of the Crown Agents in London.[48]

Despite the short-term gains made by Japan, with its cheap exports of textiles to the area, administrative and legal measures taken to combat competition were such that Kenya and Uganda — and after the First World War, Tanganyika — remained British colonies, essentially integrated into the economy of the British Empire with only peripheral competition from competitors under the Congo Basin arrangement. In the following chapters, we shall note those measures which were taken to incorporate East Africa bilaterally into the British and German economies, first showing how these powers tried to frame an economic strategy for the integration of the region, and then how this integration was achieved both vertically and horizontally.

References

1. G.A. Wainwright, 'Early Foreign Trade in East Africa', *Man*, Vol. Vol. XLVII, November 1947, p. 143, as referred to by K. Ingham, *A History of East Africa* (London, Longmans, 1966), p. 1.
2. For an account of this as far as Africa is concerned, see, for instance, W. Rodney, *How Europe Underdeveloped Africa* (London/Dar es Salaam, Bogle-L'Ouverture/Tanzania Publishing House, 1972).
3. Ingham, *op. cit.*, p. 6.
4. D.K. Fieldhouse, *The Colonial Empires* (London/New York, Weidenfeld and Nicolson, 1966), pp. 5–6.
5. L.C.A. Knowles, *The Economic Development of the British Overseas Empire* (London, George Routledge and Sons, 1924) Part 1; Fieldhouse, *op. cit.*, pp. 6–7.
6. Ingham, *op. cit.*, p. 7.
7. Ingham, *op. cit.* , p. 7.
8. Ingham, *op. cit.*, pp. 18–19.
9. Knowles, *op. cit.*, pp. 9–28.
10. See B. Semmell, *Free Trade Imperialism* (Cambridge, Cambridge University Press, 1970); see also Volume Two of the present work.
11. Knowles, *op. cit.*, p. 108.
12. Ingham, *op. cit.*, p. 23.
13. Knowles, *op. cit.*, pp. 75–6.
14. Jeremy Bentham, *Emancipate Your Colonies*, a pamphlet published in 1793; see also Adam Smith, *The Wealth of Nations*, 1776, various modern editions.
15. J.B. Condliffe, *The Commerce of Nations* (London, Allen and Unwin, 1951).
16. Quoted in A. Le R. Burt, *Evolution of the British Empire and Commonwealth* (Boston, Heath, 1956), p. 444.
17. Knowles, *op. cit.*, p. 24.
18. Ingham, *op. cit.*, pp. 28–33; see also Sir John Gray, *The British in Mombasa. 1824–26* (London, Macmillan, 1971).
19. D. Ricardo, *Principles of Political Economy and Taxation* (London, Pelican, 1971), p. 152.
20. Ingham, *op. cit.*, p. 76.
21. *Ibid.*, p. 56.
22. *Ibid.*, p. 56.
23. *Ibid.*, p. 60.
24. R. Coupland, *The Exploitation of East Africa* (London, Faber and Faber, 1968), p. 320.
25. *Ibid.*, p. 322–3.
26. *Ibid.*, pp. 321–2.
27. *Ibid.*, p. 322.

28. Quoted in D.W. Nabudere, *Imperialism and Revolution in Uganda* (London/Dar es Salaam, Onyx Press/Tanzania Publishing House, 1978), p. 28.
29. Knowles, *op. cit.*, p. 170.
30. Quoted in *ibid.*, p. 171.
31. Ingham, *op. cit.*
32. *Ibid.*, p. 88.
33. *Ibid.*, p. 104.
34. Coupland, *op. cit.*, p. 15.
35. Knowles, *op. cit.*, p. 15.
36. *Ibid.*, p. 27.
37. V.I. Lenin, *Imperialism, the Highest Stage of Capitalism* (Moscow, Progress Publishers, 1970), p. 86.
38. L.C.A. Knowles, *Economic Development in the Nineteenth Century* (London, Routledge, 1936), p. 172.
39. *Ibid.*
40. W.O. Henderson, 'German East Africa, 1884–1918' in Harlow, Chilvers and Smith (eds.), *History of East Africa*, Vol. II (London, Oxford University Press, 1965), pp. 131–2.
41. *Ibid.*, p. 134.
42. Charles Dundas, *A History of German East Africa* (Government Printer, DSM, 1923); Ingham, *op. cit.*, p. 177; see, for instance, the editor's introduction to the semi-official Oxford *History of East Africa, op. cit.*, p. xlix.
43. Ingham, *op. cit.*, pp. 137–90.
44. Lenin, *op. cit.*, p. 20.
45. Ingham, *op. cit.*, p. 181.
46. *Ibid.*, p. 127; see also G. Martelli, *Leopold to Lumumba: A History of the Belgian Congo, 1877–1960* (London, Chapman and Hall, 1962), pp. 87–107.
47. *Oscar Chinn Case*, PCIJ (1934) series A/B No. 63, p. 84.
48. E.A. Brett, *Colonialism and Underdevelopment in East Africa: The Politics of Economic Change, 1919–39* (London, Heinemann, 1973).

2. The Tanganyikan Colonial Economy

German East Africa

German East Africa, consisting of the three territories later known under the British and Belgian mandates as Tanganyika, Rwanda and Urundi, was declared a German colony in 1885. Iliffe has argued that this colonization took place for two reasons. First, it would be useful in the 'quarrel' with Britain; second, being 'ignorant' of East Africa, Germany wanted to forestall the other claimants in order to gain 'some unknown advantages' from it. Iliffe even suggests that the 'idea of conquest' can be attributed to an individual – Carl Peters.[1] In fact, the motivation for German colonization of East Africa was economic, and was rooted in the monopoly capitalist economy of Germany. Otherwise, the financial and industrial monopolies would not have invested in Carl Peters' German East African Company, the *Deutsche Ostafrika Gesellschaft* (D.O.A.G.). As we have seen, the increase in trading interests based at Zanzibar had made Germany feel herself to be the dominant imperialist power in the area. It is proof of the close link between monopoly enterprise and the imperialist state that the acquired territory was run by the D.O.A.G. on behalf of the German state until it was compelled to move in and quell the revolts against this form of domination. Rweyemamu has shown that between 1888 and 1906 there were eleven major revolts by the peasants of Tanganyika against German intrusion;[2] but these early revolts against a strong imperialist power were bound to fail and were indeed viciously crushed.

Having subdued the people and in time established a colonial administration, the Germans turned their attention to creating a colonial economy to suit their needs. This was a slow process and, in the meantime, the monopoly bourgeoisie had to content itself with what booty it could get from the interior.[3] Between 1891 and 1906 the first Governor, Julius von Soden, worked towards establishing conditions for an effective economy. Like their British counterparts, the German imperialists had to eliminate what remained of the slave trade on the coast and the hinterland. Then a compromise was struck with the powers of the pre-colonial social structure by making indigenous officials agents of the new German administration as *liwalis* (coastal governors) or *akidas* (hinterland agents). The local headmen (*jumbes*) in the villages shared some of the powers of *akidas*. As part of the strategy for eliminating the slave trade, Dar es Salaam was made the main trading port in place of the traditional port, Bagamoyo, and a German rupee was introduced instead of the Mombasa and Zanzibar rupees. These moves effectively shifted the trade routes. Zanzibar's pre-eminence as an entrepot centre was considerably reduced in favour of German ports, now linked to German agents in Indian ports and strengthened through a subsidized shipping line, *Ost-Afrika Linie*, which extended its direct service from Dar es Salaam to Aden and Bombay, bypassing Zanzibar.

The second step was to survey all the available resources in the country, as the basis for planning a colonial economy.[4] The annual reports of the colony indicate that its topography, geology, climate, plant and animal species were closely investigated. The destruction of the slave trade and the integration of the country into the German imperial system meant the construction of new communications systems with the countryside, the building of roads, a railway, a floating dock at Dar es Salaam, as well as the introduction of lighters and river vessels.

White Settlement and the Colonial Economy

The next move was to encourage commodity production. At first, no clear policy emerged as to whether and where white settlement should be encouraged or whether the African peasant should be the basis of the colonial economy. In fact, white settlement, on a very limited scale, and African peasant smallholding production co-existed.

This was necessary if the expenses of the colony were to be met. Initially, before crop production was introduced, the administration required the African people to continue hunting for ivory and collecting beeswax and wild rubber; tax was levied in kind, just as in British Uganda and Kenya. But by the 1890s sisal, cotton, rubber, groundnuts and coffee were being cultivated, to reduce Germany's dependence upon North American and Mexican sources. Some new varieties of seed were introduced by missionaries bent on encouraging 'new industry' — for instance the Arabica strain of coffee, encouraged in Kiliminjaro — though the existence of native varieties of coffee among the Bahaya also helped the development of an African coffee industry.

To speed up the supply of these products — particularly cotton, which was proving an expensive import from the U.S. — the German imperialists introduced a corvée system of labour based on communal cultivation, under which the *akidas* coerced labourers to work on large communal farms. At the end of each season the produce was divided between the marketing organization, the *akida* and the workers, each receiving one-third of the returns. This cruel exploitation was naturally resisted by the people, in the famous *Maji Maji* rebellion of 1905, which lasted two years (and provided the basis for the subsequent so-called era of 'reform'). By 1904, although ivory accounted for about two-fifths of the colony's exports, African crops made up a significant share as well.

White settlement and agriculture grew very slowly, and were restricted mainly to the Usambara, Tanga and Moshi areas, later to be known as Tanganital. Settlement in Africa had encouraged early debates in Germany about the need to have colonies, and right-wing forces, backed by the National Liberals and the Catholic *Zentrum* in the Reichstag, supported German emigration as a safety valve against social unrest;[5] nonetheless, opinion was divided as to what type of settler should be encouraged to emigrate.[6] While the conservatives argued that the settlers should be small-scale peasants on the 'Polish model', the National Liberals argued that the settlers should be men of capital — young sons of merchants and industrialists, retired officers and, especially, the Prussian lower nobility.[7] The *Zentrum* was ambivalent, fearing that such settlement would 'harm African interests'.

The policy followed by the new Governor, Renchenberg, reflecting these 'African' interests, at first did not favour white settlement, and instead encouraged peasant production based on the gradual expansion and reform of the existing indigenous agriculture.(This policy was later to be known as the 'Nyamwezi and peanuts policy'.) A market was assured by the successful completion of the Uganda Railway, which reached Kisumu in 1901. The result was a rapid development of production in indigenous crops, which could be sold for certain monopoly interests, backed by the 'Nyamwezi and peanuts policy'.

> Contemporary observers were astonished by its effects on the region of German East Africa south and west of the Lake. As soon as transport linked them to the market, the peoples of this area began to expand their output of indigenous products and to sell their surplus crops to the Indian merchants of Mwanza and Bukoba, who exported them to the coast and thence to the Indian Ocean trading area.[8]

This increased production and export, explained by the level of the tax demands, convinced the Germans of the need to construct a railway of their own to stop the products going to Uganda, where the British were in control. A decision was made to build the central line from Dar es Salaam to Tabora, 'to the Nyamwezi and peanuts . . . immediately'.[9] In the areas of the *Maji Maji* rebellion, coercion on the communal farms was no longer necessary, indeed was counter-productive. Production increases indicated that commodity production for the capitalist imperialist market was taking root as the best incentive for integrating the region to German metropolitan economy.

But these were not the only developments which had an impact on the rate and numbers of white settlement. The National Liberals, and the section of German finance capital they represented, favoured a policy of integration based on large plantation agriculture. Such a policy, they argued, would be effective in combating the undercapacity and short-time working in the German domestic textile industry, in part caused and exacerbated by Germany's dependence on the United States for cotton, and particularly by the arbitrary price manipulations of the American quasi-monopolists.[10]

Between 1897 and 1906, the average price of American raw cotton in Hamburg was 70 Pf. per kg. In February 1904 it was 170 Pf. and in December the same year it fell to 70 Pf., while in September 1907, after a heavy crop, the price was still as high as 120 Pf.[11] Consequently, cotton-growing in the colonies was encouraged and a Colonial Economic Committee to promote the growth of cotton and other raw materials was formed under the leadership of a Nuremberg textile manufacturer. When the indigenous response was not enthusiastic, monopoly interests in textiles began to remedy this lag by large-scale plantation of cotton. By 1907 12 companies were in the field with 125,000 acres in the Sadani area.[12]

Early efforts at plantation agriculture in coffee and sisal were unsuccessful. Coffee production recovered after the 1910 boom in coffee prices on the world market; and in 1911-12 the largest company in the field paid its first dividend on a coffee plantation. In Meru and Kilimanjaro large plantations were in evidence. But sisal declined: although one of the largest sisal companies had paid a dividend of 7% between 1905 and 1907, the situation worsened with the overall fall in prices between 1902 and 1911, giving more room to small estate companies and individual settlers.

A new opening for large companies occurred in the plantation of rubber, which by 1907 was starting to pay well. With the high prices of 1909 and 1910, new capital moved in to tap this resource where labour was so cheap. Rubber became the 'magnet of the world's speculative capital, temporarily supplanting gold and oil'.[13] The British, who were the biggest rubber speculators, investing £36 million in the first half of 1910, sank some of this capital in large plantations in German East Africa, opening up 40,000 acres by November that year and buying a number of plantation lands from German settlers. Although this boom had collapsed by 1913, the price of sisal was then rising again, with coffee close behind, so that plantation and settler agriculture maintained itself right up to the end of the German period.

By 1912 German East Africa had attracted 4,866 European settlers and officials, largely through its plantation policy. One advantage of the policy was that a high level of expatriate settlement relieved Germany of some of the unemployment pressure at home. Another was that capital which had no outlets at home could be profitably exported, while markets were created at home and in the colonies for various products. Finally German imperialism was assured of access to strategic materials like sisal which, although expensive to produce, enabled Germany to supply its navy with cordage independently of British supplies. There were also disadvantages.[14] Among these was the very high level of capitalization: as it turned out, much capital invested in sisal and cotton plantations was never recouped after the interruption of operations at the outbreak of war in 1914.

In fact, peasant agriculture remained the most viable method of low-cost production for most raw material products, including those grown on large estates. Governor Renchenberg, commenting on the 'reform era' in 1907, said:

> I have gained the impression that East Africa's economy cannot be
> based on the activities of plantations and settlers . . . that this land must
> be developed through its indigenous products, through the natural
> experience of its native inhabitants, and that, despite all solicitude for
> European capital, the development of the native economy is the surest
> way to a broadly designed colonial policy.[15]

This period thus saw further encouragement to African peasant agriculture
but with a difference — it was found expedient to rely on the Indian trader
as the new intermediary for German finance capital.

The Role of the Asian Trader

Indian merchants had been present in this part of the world even before the
Arabs and the Portuguese, trading along the East Coast. When India came
under British control, their role in the area was increasingly subordinated to
the needs of British imperialism as Britain built up its hegemony against
French and German competition. With German colonization of East Africa,
however, and the consequent shifting of the trade routes, the Indian retail
trader found a new position which Renchenberg came to see as essential to
the 'Nyamwezi and peanuts policy'.'He [Renchenberg] encouraged Indian
retail trading, against criticism, because the traders were the essential inter-
mediaries between producers and their markets.'[16]

With African producers, Indian traders and the local railway, peanuts
and other crops could be produced, bought and transported, and the cheap
manufactured goods bought by the indigenous population, all to the advantage of German industry. By 1910 there were 6,723 Asian traders in German
East Africa, taking up residence in small centres further in the interior as
security improved. Their ambiguous legal status was ideal: as British subjects
they were aliens and therefore easily controllable; on the other hand, since
their customs did not entitle them to be subject to German private law, they
were legally regarded as natives.[17] Although small capitalist settler elements
regarded them as a competitive threat, the big monopoly bourgeoisie, who
had the general interests of German finance capital at heart, ignored such
petty-bourgeois prejudices. By the end of German rule there were well-
articulated intermediary relationships between the Asian traders and the
Deutsche Ostafrika Gesellschaft. It has been suggested by some writers that
the Asian traders played the role of 'price giver', to the African role of
'price taker';[18] but on the whole it was the German monopolies which governed the conditions of production, and of trade, and hence prices. Although
the Asians might in many cases have cheated the African consumers by
setting prices above those fixed by the D.O.A.G., the basic relations on
which the economy operated as a whole were those of monopoly capitalism.
And these relations obviously included setting price above cost.

Integration and the D.O.A.G.

The integration of East Africa into German imperialism was entirely effected by the monopoly activities of the D.O.A.G. This monopoly made a fortune out of compensation paid to it by the German imperial state for its so-called 'losses' incurred in the colonization of the territory for German imperialism. During the colonial period it prospered as production expanded, gaining new land concessions and controlling large plantations, a wide trading network and the only two banks in the territory. Its control of the banks meant that the entire mortgage business of the territory passed through its hands, with the result that it owned by lien most non-governmental buildings and other structures.[19] The D.O.A.G. monopoly over trading activities in the territory consisted not only in buying the entire crop of cotton and rubber but also in handling most of the region's import business.[20] Indeed, most Asian traders were its direct agents. Between 1905 and 1913 it made a net profit of seven million marks.[21] From 1906 to 1908, it paid dividends of 5%; in 1909, 6%; in 1910 and 1911, 8% and in 1912, 9%. Shares in the D.O.A.G., offered on the Berlin Bourse in 1909, reached a 50% premium within nine months. The company's local manager had a seat on East Africa's Advisory Council,[22] assuring close political links between the D.O.A.G. and the German Government.

The D.O.A.G.'s monopoly of production and trade in East Africa, and the control it exercised over administrative processes, in close co-operation with the German Government, created the conditions for bilateral imperialism in the territory. Despite the provisions of the Congo Basin treaties, almost all incoming capital originated in Germany. By 1911, 59% of the territory's exports went to Germany, compared with 22% in 1897, when 72% went to British hands through the Zanzibar entrepot. In 1911 only 10% went to British ports through Zanzibar.[23] Imports from Germany included railway equipment, machinery, vehicles and instruments. Only the importing of textiles was left to foreign merchants as a means of raising the 'German element in the colonies'.[24] East Africa under German domination expanded its range of exports to include about 17 agricultural and mineral products, while the destinations of these exports shrank correspondingly, and were eventually limited to Germany alone.[25] At the same time, the sources of imports to East Africa narrowed to one — Germany — while their content and variety gradually grew as the economy developed.

Overall, at the end of the German period there was 'a fairly vigorous development' both of the infrastructure and of agriculture, plantation and peasant, all 'stimulated by a massive capital inflow'.[26] Before it was lost to British imperialism the territory ranked third out of the seven German colonies, after Kiautschou and South West Africa.

Britain Takes an Interest
Between 1897 and 1912 exports from German East Africa ranged from 36.4% to 63.0% of imports, indicating a high degree of capital import. The territory was now a 'commercial venture — capital on private account' — with a local budget being met from local taxes. Yaffey has observed:

By 1912 the private capital inflow appears to have reached the astonishing level of over 40% of imports . . . By modern standards the investors appear to have been venturesome and to have had high expectations. The profit in 1912 was in fact about MK. 3.8 Mn., representing 12% of exports, some three times higher than the figure today. Moreover, head office expenses included a form of profit.[27]

The success of this venture in colonization drew the attention of the more experienced British imperialists, who, in the words of their Governor in neighbouring Kenya, noted that whereas the British had concentrated on railway building and had shown 'extreme parsimony and indifference [sic] in other respects', the Germans had done 'little' in the way of railway construction, but, on the contrary, had devoted themselves to the 'methodical development of the colony with systematic thoroughness . . . and lavishment due to the determination to establish a colonial empire at any price'.[28] Such was the prize that German imperialism had won in the scramble — and it was paying.

Table 1
Imports and Exports of German East Africa, 1906–12 (million marks)

	1906	1907	1908	1909	1910	1911	1912
Imports	25.2	23.8	25.8	33.9	38.7	45.9	50.3
Exports	11.0	12.5	10.9	13.1	20.8	22.4	31.4
Total	*36.2*	*36.3*	*37.7*	*47.0*	*59.5*	*68.3*	*81.7*

Source: W.O. Henderson, in Harlow, Chilvers and Smith, *History of East Africa, op. cit.,* p. 153.

It is not surprising, therefore, that in the rivalry between Britain and Germany in this period a war for redivision should have broken out in 1914, and that the British should have immediately entertained the idea of colonizing German East Africa for themselves. The immediate effect of the British naval blockade on the territory was an outbreak of '*ersatz* production' for civilian and military purposes. The establishment of the research station at Amani facilitated the local manufacture and production of a number of new commodities — an experiment in industrialization that was never to be repeated. Sixteen varieties of food and liquors, 11 spices, 12 kinds of medicine and medicament, 5 varieties of rubber product, 2 of soap, plus other goods such as oils and candles, went into production within the space of three years.[29] These developments merely sustained German East Africa in the brief period of its blockade, after which Britain, a new imperialist power, moved in to integrate the territory with its own economy.

Tanganyika Under British Imperialism

The cession of Tanganyika to the British came about as the result of the First World War — a war that was waged in order to decide whether Britain or Germany was to obtain the opportunity and the right to rob, strangle and exploit the whole world.[30] If the battle was decided in favour of the British allies, it was only to raise even more acutely the contradictions within imperialism as a system of exploitation and oppression. It was not long before Britain's hegemony was to be destroyed by another war which, although nominally a victory, effectively rendered her a second-rate imperialist power.

Whatever the future held in store, in 1918 British imperialism moved at once to incorporate Tanganyika, as it now came to be called, under her own control. Using international mechanisms, it obtained the right to administer and exploit Tanganyika as an 'integral part of the mandatory power and its dependencies'.[31] Under Article 10 of the mandate Britain obtained the right to 'constitute the territory into a customs union, fiscal and administrative union or federation with the adjacent territories under [its] own sovereignty or control', subject to the provisions of the mandate.[32] Once effective occupation of the territory was established, 'alien Germans' were refused permission to restore their firms to production, and were expelled, to enable settlement by British or allied citizens. This opportunity was seized upon by many Greeks, who moved into sisal plantations, formerly owned by Germans on annual leases.[33]

Having obtained the territory free of all German-incurred public debt, plus the right to acquire basic infrastructures at nominal cost, Britain set out to integrate Tanganyika bilaterally with its own economy, in many cases acting against the provisions of Article 7 of the mandate regarding equality of opportunity for all members of the League of Nations. Competing products from countries like Japan, for instance, were excluded from the territory.

The transition period was relatively smooth, for the British made no radical changes to the administrative and legal structures, preferring as far as possible to adapt existing institutions. At the ideological level, both Britain and Germany hoped to discredit each other by exposing brutality, the use of forced labour and other malpractices of which both sides had certainly been guilty;[34] but these propaganda battles merely masked each power's true intention — to strengthen its influence in the territory.

A further step in the integration of Tanganyika was to reinstate the silver rupee, whose sterling value fluctuated with the London silver price.[35] In 1921 Tanganyika, together with neighbouring Kenya and Uganda, came under the scope of the newly created East African Currency Board, just one of several regional institutions which — as we shall see later — served to provide horizontal integration of East Africa.

The first administrative measures included in the Tanganyika Order in Council of 22 July 1920 was the creation of the office of Governor and Commander-in-Chief. This officer headed the colony, with the assistance of an Executive Council and a High Court. The 22 administrative districts of the earlier regime were retained, as well as the services of the experienced *akidas*, on a reduced basis. This limited revival of old forms of indigenous institutions, altered to serve the needs of British imperialist power, was accomplished under Governor Cameron and institutionalized through the Native Authorities Ordinance of 1921. New laws based on Indian codes and procedures were introduced, to be supplemented by English statutes and common law, but customary law was also recognized to some extent.

A Shaky Start
British efforts to make the territory immediately productive were thwarted for some 10 years by the after-effects of the war. Famine conditions prevailed in many places and both African peasant agriculture and white settler plantations were 'practically derelict'. Communications had been demobilized, and many roads were 'nothing but caravan tracks'.[36] Rehabilitation work had to be undertaken, law and order re-established and 'friendly and close contact' made with the peasantry 'before any programme of development could be started'.[37] The inauguration of such a programme was also held up by mutual imperialist mistrust, some of it generated by the Germans still in the territory and by others outside, who spread rumours that the British presence was soon to be superseded by a new German victory.[38] In Britain itself there were fears that mandated territories might change hands and property titles be made worthless.[39] When these rumours came to the attention of Governor Cameron, he reassured would-be investors that 'all discussion as to the possibility of Tanganyika Territory, or any part of it, passing from British control is superfluous and has to be deprecated'.[40]

Despite these reassurances very little private capital came in. Even the official grants-in-aid, loan grants and bonds guaranteed by the British Treasury at high rates of interest amounted to no more than 7% of total imports in 1938, as compared to 40% in 1912 when the territory was under German domination.[41] By 1940, and the Second World War, uncertainty over the territory still prevailed, with the result that the Government Central Committee was constrained to remark in its Report of that year that, despite the 'interlude of comparatively good prices' between 1935 and 1938, 'non-native enterprise was seriously impeded by widespread uncertainty regarding the political future of Tanganyika as a mandated territory'. The Report added: 'This uncertainty, we must trust, and believe, has now been finally dispelled, but its retarding effect on development was enormous and to a large extent explains the absence of spectacular progress during recent years, for it naturally led to reluctance to invest sorely needed capital in the territory.'[42]

The Production Policy Takes Shape
Despite the rather discouraging tone of the Report, it also noted that 'nevertheless in spite of these disabilities', progress in exports was 'by no means discouraging'. Some of the explanation for this must be seen in the

coercive methods used under the labour laws against African plantation workers, and the exploitation of the poor peasantry working their individual plots. Systematic exploitation took place in four main stages.[43] First was the stage of 'optimistic land development' in the early period of the mandate, when new crops of cotton and Arabica coffee were investigated at the old German centres. Despite the opposition of the white settlers in Kilimanjaro region, peasant production of coffee was established as the only form of production to promise quick returns. Other peasant crops which were encouraged included groundnuts, sesame, rice, hides and skins and ghee, while sisal saw a great increase in the Southern Highlands.

The Tanganyika Land Ordinance of 1923 declared public all land except the existing freehold titles. From then on land was leased for periods not exceeding 99 years. Non-Africans were not entitled to occupy more than 5,000 acres of land without the approval of the Colonial Secretary. To achieve increased production, a higher level of taxation was introduced in 1925. 'Administrative persuasion' — and in some cases (such as the cotton plantations, whose produce was so much in demand by British textile interests) physical coercion — had to be used to enforce it. The inter-war years had placed British imperialists in a position, analogous to that of the Germans at the beginning of their colonial period, of having to defend their commercial interests by force.[44]

Thus the end of this period of land exploitation saw the re-establishment of the old dual economy of plantation and peasant production. Under the Native Master and Servant Ordinance of 1923, the settlers being assured of a large labour force from the demobilized African Carrier Corps. By 1929 African production accounted for exports to the value of £1,475,078, while European production was valued in the same period at £1,877,421. The Kilimanjaro Native Planters' Association was formed in 1924 as a union of coffee growers (later it became a co-operative union), and the Tanganyika Sisal Growers' Association was also formed by white settlers as a pressure group.

During this period, too, British imperialists tried to improve employment opportunities at home by encouraging investment in the colonies. In Tanganyika this took the concrete form of creating infrastructure by extending the railway system, thus using British steel and engineering expertise; moreover, the railways were directed to areas where crops like cotton could be grown, again creating employment in the home textile manufacturing sector. The consequent improvement in Britain's balance of payments would, it was hoped, bring the pound to parity with the U.S. dollar, strengthening Britain's position in the world market. In this respect the Colonial Development Act of 1929 merely consolidated the efforts advanced by the Loans Acts of 1924 and 1926 in this direction. The Colonial Stocks Act was also amended to bring protectorates and mandated territories like Tanganyika under their provisions, enabling the raising of capital for these developments. Tanganyika, 'worst hit by the Depression', had a large share (over 60%) of the funds assigned to East Africa for the development of railways, roads and irrigation, and for surveying.[45] The loans raised under the various Loans Acts provided for the construction of the Tabora–Mwanza line (1928) and the Moshi–Arusha line (1929).

'Plant More Crops'
The second phase of development under British rule was to a large extent conditioned by the Depression of the 1930s. Prices of agricultural products fell; peasants accordingly abandoned cash crops to concentrate on subsistence farming. The government's reaction was to launch a campaign to 'Plant More Crops' among peasants cultivating cotton. Despite the coercive measures which accompanied this drive, and despite the resultant increase in yield of up to 30% for coffee and cotton, declining prices produced export earnings below the pre-1929 levels. As a result, imports to the territory were reduced and this meant a loss of customs revenue. With low wages the peasants could not afford to buy even the 'astonishingly cheap Japanese goods which were flooding the market'[46] and reverted to clothing made from bark cloth and skin.

Without cheap labour the plantation economy would have collapsed entirely. Although forced to economize drastically, the settlers still maintained their plantations, and continued to increase their output. The Report of the Central Development Committee, already cited, noted in 1940: 'There can be no doubt that without the stabilizing factor of capital invested in the country there would have been almost complete disruption of the Territory's economic and social structure, inevitably leading to a fall in the African's standard of living from what was then little more than a tax-paying level to a bare subsistence basis.'[47]

In fact, not only did the standard of living for most African peasants return to near-subsistence level, the production of coffee and cotton, which had shown an increase with the 'Plant More Crops' campaign, went to bolster up the British economy. Moreover, it was the cheap African labour force which had to accept increasingly lower wages in this period; this was the only way that the white capitalist settlers were saved from reducing their own standard of living to subsistence level. The sisal crop which, according to Iliffe, 'followed exactly the fortunes of the American economy', fell in price from £32 per ton in 1929 to £11 in 1932.[48] Output, however, did not fall — indeed it was increased through increased labour input. Yet this increase in productivity was accompanied by an actual decrease in wages between 1930 and 1932, from Shs. 36 to Shs. 10 per task.[49]

Depression and Diversification
The third stage in the Tanganyikan colonial economy began in 1934, in the wake of the Depression. Activities to integrate the area more closely with the British economy took the form of diversifying crop production. New crops such as fire- and flue-cured coffee were introduced, as well as sugar cane, pyrethrum, papain and wheat on a plantation scale. At the same time, greater production of a range of crops suitable for small-scale production was

also encouraged, with crops such as sesame, groundnuts, cashew nuts, citrus fruits and onions.[50] Soil conservation was encouraged and new agricultural research centres opened.

With the outbreak of the Second World War all production – except, for once, cotton production – was geared up for the war effort. This meant increased pressure on the peasant growers, and in 1937, in the coffee-producing Bukoba area, they rioted in protest at the low prices paid to them. The demand to increase sisal production required ever more coercive administrative and legal measures, including the contract system with its heavy bias in favour of the capitalist farmer. By 1945 the political consciousness of the people was beginning to be mobilized against this seemingly endless exploitation in the cash crop areas and the first demands for peasant control of marketing were made. The fact that it was the emergent class of rich peasants who originated these demands reflected the uneven development resulting from Britain's intervention in the economy. The separation of export-producing, food-producing and labour-supplying areas could only divide the people and serve the interests of British finance capital.[51]

Yet this intensive level of exploitation could not be maintained. Despite efforts to conserve the soil, it was being badly eroded and, consequently, less productive. Equally, the pressing demands made on the peasants to grow more crops eroded the amount of time and energy for growing their own food. Yet the pressure was kept up: complaints by British finance capital that peasant agriculture was unable to provide enough oil and fats for the depleted post-war British market led to the initiation of the ill-fated Groundnut Scheme in 1946. When this grandiose scheme failed, at a cost of £35,870,000, the colonial state finally shifted production back to the peasants. A number of rehabilitation schemes were set up throughout the country. These measures, designed to supply Britain with goods in peace-time as well as in war, were now called 'colonial and welfare development'. Actually, apart from the consumer needs of the British population, Britain needed dollar-earning cash crops to enable it to repay U.S. loans contracted during and just after the war. By the end of the war, however, Tanganyikan agricultural production was highly integrated with the British economy, and with that of the Empire; over half of all its exports went to other colonies. As far as imports were concerned, the bulk came from the sterling area, followed by Japan. In this period the bulk purchasing system, controlled by the British and colonial states, was introduced to enable Britain to satisfy her needs at the cheapest possible price during war years.

Post-War Rationalization

The fourth and last period began with the devaluation of the British pound in 1949 and British efforts to save all the dollars possible to repay money borrowed from the U.S. under the various borrowing schemes, such as the Lend-Lease agreement. Here efforts were made to 'plan' colonial development and to appease and neutralize the growing opposition which accompanied increased political awareness among Africans. But, of course, the Colonial

Development and Welfare Act was in imperialist interests, intended to strengthen Britain's trading position.[52] In Tanganyika British imperialism had already scored major victories over the toiling people, the value of exports far exceeding the paltry capital investment in the territory.

Peace-time, however, meant a change. The Government's Central Development Committee, whose activities had been interrupted by the war, resumed its work and produced *An Outline of Post-War Development Proposals*, a plan which embodied a framework within which future developments could be formulated after the war. The Central Committee recommended an expenditure of nearly £9 million over 10 years to increase agricultural and mineral production.[53] Attention was given particularly to the provision of agricultural credit. A Land Bank was formed in 1948 with initial capital of Shs. 4 million, later increased to Shs. 6 million, to be taken from the revenues of the territory. Between 1948 and 1960, 32% of these funds were used, mainly by the settlers, to buy land and discharge debts, 28% went into annual cultivation and crop marketing, and 40% went towards long-term agricultural development. This policy, together with the land tenure policies advocated by the East African Royal Commission, consolidated the emergence of a rich African peasantry ('progressive' farmers) as a definite grouping in Kilimanjaro, West Lake, Mbulu, South Highlands and other regions. It was this class which led the co-operative and later political movements. Government policy now emphasized research activities, with a view to increasing the productivity of smallholding agriculture. More capital investment was also encouraged by the importation of new machinery and equipment for plantation agriculture; credit was extended to both sectors of agriculture to enable further investment; and, in order to contain the political activities of the peasantry, co-operative marketing was allowed.

The soil conservation and land rehabilitation schemes began to pay dividends - particularly the Uluguru Land Usage Scheme, the Mbulu Development Plan and the Sukumaland Development Scheme. The last of these, which aimed at redistributing the human and animal population from crowded areas of northern and central Sukumaland - Mwanza and Kwimba - to less densely populated areas in the south - Geita, Maswa and Shinyanga - (at a cost of £2,000) succeeded in moving some 30,000 people to Geita District within five years, leading to a fivefold increase in cotton output between 1947 and 1961.[54] When many of these schemes provoked the poor peasantry to resist, British finance capital stepped up its policy of establishing the rich peasant as a safety valve in the countryside. A number of commissions were appointed to ensure the implementation of this policy, culminating in The East Africa Royal Commission of 1953-5, which recommended altering the land tenure system so as to enable rich peasants and capitalist farmers to raise credit on the basis of the security of their land titles. This scheme, though accepted by the Tanganyika Government, was condemned by the Tanganyika African National Union, which had by then come into existence as the country's nationalist movement.

Nevertheless, all these plans resulted in a steady development of agriculture,

most of it destined for export. Whereas in 1945 the gross exports from the
country were barely £6,215,000, by the end of 1960 they amounted to
£41,000,000, partly as a result of a large increase in the acreage devoted to
cotton cultivation in the West Lake region – from 142,000 acres in 1945 to
582,000 acres in 1960. Land under sisal cultivation increased over the same
period from 448,784 to 664,482 acres.[55] On the large estates, farming
became mechanized and employment declined. While the production of sisal
rose by about 85% between 1945 and 1960, adult employment increased
only slightly; while for plantation coffee the increase of 200% in production
attracted only a 33% increase in employment, and for tea the increase of
500% in production led to an increase of only 100% in employment.[56]
Fuggles-Couchman has commented: 'These figures reflect the tremendous
increase in the use of mechanical equipment wherever possible, of better
labour usage, and to some degree of better field practices giving higher
returns per acre.'[57]

Like the Germans, the British ensured the structural integration of the
territory with a chain of financial institutions and banks, merchandizing
houses, insurance firms, warehouses and shipping lines. The fact that many
of these companies had their headquarters in Nairobi illustrates the way in
which the process of British bilateral integration could incorporate a whole
region as a market. The Asian traders still played an intermediary role, from
which the African trader and the rich peasant struggled to supplant them.
The marketing of the sisal crop was almost entirely handled by brokers, the
most important being Ralli Brothers, a British monopoly associated with Sir
Isaac Wolfson's financial and trading empire. The firm handled all sisal
purchasing, transport, warehousing, insurance and shipping. Coffee and
cotton, which had been sold at auction by agents such as Tancot Ltd. and
Brooke Bond, were marketed during and after the war by the British state
itself. Bulk-purchasing contracts on both sides ensured 'a steady flow of
essential commodities to the United Kingdom', as a way of 'assisting the
United Kingdom in her war effort'. In the absence of such arrangements,
the United Kingdom, according to Leubuscher, 'might not have been able
to obtain supplies which she needed or might have been compelled to pay
excessive prices or to pay in dollars or other hard currencies rather than in
sterling'.[58]

In this way Tanganyikan coffee, cotton and sisal, 'which became of vital
strategic importance for the Allies',[59] were sold by the Tanganyikan Government, using local agents for internal marketing, and by the British Ministry
of Food, which managed the bulk purchases on the British side. In addition,
the government in Tanganyika, taking advantage of very high prices for
coffee, was able to retain as price stabilization funds considerable sums of
money which were never paid back to the peasants. It is estimated that the
peasant producers lost £11,000,000 in this way. These funds were capitalized by the state and put to use for 'development' projects, including
research and construction of public works and infrastructure, reducing the
dependence on imported capital for those purposes. The internal purchasing

33

agents of the colonial state were the same buying monopolies that had operated in the country before the war, and were thus (as in West Africa) able to strengthen their financial position further.[60]

Bulk purchasing at the end of the war provided the basis for more permanent state involvement in the marketing of cash crops, in the form of Marketing Boards. In Tanganyika a Lint and Seed Marketing Board was set up in 1952 to replace the bulk-purchasing system; its main function was to purchase the lint from ginneries. Although coffee reverted to private auctioning in 1954, most of it went to co-operative marketing bodies as the co-operatives increasingly took over this function. Sisal reverted to private marketing for export for the larger estates (which handled 48% of the crop), and to joint marketing for the smaller estates (which handled 52% of the crop) from 1949 onwards.

After 1950 many exports from the territory were deliberately sent to non-sterling areas to earn dollars for Britain to pay off her debts; most of the sisal, for instance, went to the United States. By this process Tanganyika was beginning to multilateralize her exports. Slowly but surely, Britain's hegemony was giving way to the new system we shall be examining in more detail in later chapters. Exports in this period also rose sharply in price, affected by the devaluation of the pound in 1949 and the Korean War boom. Little of this increase in prices reached the growers, since the state removed it in the form of taxes; it was, in fact, the resulting wave of political agitation which led to the formation of the national movement for Tanganyika's independence.

In this period the improved trading surpluses were still directed to imports from the sterling areas.[61] The same trading monopolies which handled Tanganyika's exports dealt also with its imports. Private importing was handled by British monopoly firms like Smith Mackenzie and Dalgety. The Inchcape Group, one of the largest trading monopolies in the world, handled imports for a number of British monopolies on an exclusive marketing basis. Government imports were handled by the Crown Agents for the colonial state. At the retail level, the Asian traders continued to be an asset, and, on the basis of 90-day credit arrangements with the British monopoly banks, distributed the products to the consumer. This link between monopoly manufacturing firms in Britain and local trading monopolies in Africa, using exclusive marketing agreements and purchases through the Crown Agents (and later also through INTRATA), allowed imports to be overpriced whenever local purchasing power was 'unusually high',[62] and to be sold at normal monopoly prices whenever purchasing power was low. In this way the 'abnormal purchasing power' earned in the peak period of 1951–4 was siphoned off to Britain,[63] rather than being used for local development.

Thus the development of colonial production in no way entailed colonial industrialization. At the point of production in the colony, raw materials were processed only so far as to reduce their bulk for export. The interests of imperialist/finance capital were best served by the colonies' remaining sources of cheap raw materials and consumers of surplus, overpriced, or redundant manufactured goods. This principle was not openly expressed;

instead the colonial bureaucracy often argued that local manufacturing
would reduce customs revenue on the imported products.

The implicit defence of the interests of British monopoly and finance
capitalism was underwritten by the Governors of Tanganyika and Uganda in
their statement at the Governors' conference in Nairobi in 1953. It was
agreed then that industrialization would be permitted in these territories only
in relation to agricultural production, and then only if it was not solely for
export purposes or if it would result in 'profitable employment' in agriculture 'to so large a proportion of the local population that the resultant
prosperity is likely to make a substantial contribution to economic welfare'.[64]
Official despatches from the Colonial Office to the Governors reflect this
approach, making it clear that the aims of the colonial state apparatus and of
British monopoly capital were at one.

Thus, in conformity with the Governors' resolution, virtually no industrialization of any significance took place in Tanganyika. A meat-processing
plant was established only because the export of beef products to the United
States would bolster British earnings. A Japanese monopoly which wanted
to invest in a match factory at Tanga was frustrated by the Colonial Office,
on the grounds that schemes of this sort 'might have serious results if carried
out in the East African territories'.[65] Another industrial project, the manufacture of sisal twine, was suppressed as soon as it threatened the position of
the home industry. Early in the 1930s three factories were set up to manufacture binder twine for export, in order to take advantage of the mooted
imperial preference system. In this case production was allowed since it was
judged not to interfere with the exportable surplus; nevertheless, as the
exports began to compete with the products of British manufacturers, the
British Rope Twine and Netmakers' Federation protested and threatened not
to buy Tanganyikan sisal. The Colonial Office was forced to impose a heavy
duty on the importing of Tanganyika-produced twine in order to protect the
British manufacturers and Tanganyikan sisal producers. As a result the
Tanganyikan production of twine stopped entirely in 1938.

Thus, despite the fact that the sisal processing industry had been established with British capital, because it contradicted the *general* interest of
British finance capital *as a whole*, it had to be disowned. It was made quite
clear in the House of Commons that 'all goods manufactured by native labour
within the Colonial Empire' would be debarred from the British market and
that 'the great interest of the colonies is to secure markets for their *primary*
products'.[66] This was not to be entirely true for Kenya, where on occasion
it suited the general interests of British finance capital in its bilateral markets
to encourage some industrialization. Essentially, however, Tanganyika was
integrated as primary producer. Manufacturing activities at the time of
independence were restricted to certain types of secondary agricultural
processing such as grain- and oil-milling, and to the production of food and
beverages. Other permitted activities were carpentry, furniture production
and saw-milling, motor vehicle repair and general engineering (including
the repair workshops of the East African Railways at Dar es Salaam).[67]

At the end of the colonial period manufacturing accounted for barely 4% of Tanganyika's gross domestic product. Most of the import substitution industrialization which occurred in the East African region did not find its way to Tanganyika. Very little capital entered the country, partly for the historical reasons given earlier and partly because new capital tended to flow instead to Kenya. Unlike Uganda, which relied on peasant earnings, Tanganyika could not even find new sources of revenue, and this tended to create imbalance and strain among the three territories, even under colonial rule.

References

1. J. Iliffe, 'Tanganyika under German and British Rule' in J. Saul and L. Cliffe (eds.), *Socialism in Tanzania*, Vol. I, Nairobi, East Africa Publishing House, 1972), p. 8.
2. J.F. Rweyemamu, *Underdevelopment and Industrialization in Tanzania* (Nairobi, Oxford University Press, 1973), pp. 12–13.
3. W.O. Henderson, 'German East Africa, 1884–1918' in Harlow, Chilvers and Smith (eds.), *History of East Africa* (London, Oxford University Press, 1965), p. 142.
4. W. Rodney, 'The Political Economy of Colonial Tanganyika, 1890–1906', paper presented to the History Teachers Conference, Morogoro, 15–21 June 1974.
5. J. Iliffe, *Tanganyika under German Rule, 1905–1912* (Nairobi, East Africa Publishing House, 1973), p. 41.
6. *Ibid.*, pp. 56–64.
7. *Ibid.*, pp. 56–64,
8. *Ibid.*, p. 71.
9. *Ibid.*, p. 72.
10. *Ibid.*, p. 77.
11. *Ibid.*, p. 76.
12. *Ibid.*, p. 78.
13. *Ibid.*, pp. 100–1.
14. Rweyemamu, *op. cit.*, pp. 23–5.
15. Quoted in Iliffe, *Tanganyika, op. cit.*, p. 24.
16. *Ibid.*, p. 76.
17. *Ibid.*, p. 94.
18. I. Shivji, *Class Struggles in Tanzania* (Dar es Salaam, Heinemann/Tanzania Publishing House, 1975), p. 42.
19. Iliffe, *Tanganyika, op. cit.*, p. 97.
20. Rweyemamu, *op. cit.*, p. 32.
21. Rodney, *op. cit.*, p. 13.
22. Iliffe, *Tanganyika, op. cit.*, p. 97.
23. M.J.F. Yaffey, *Balance of Payments Problems of a Developing Country: Tanzania* (Munich, Welt Forum Verlag, 1968), p. 45.
24. *Ibid.*
25. Rweyamamu, *op. cit.*, p. 15.

26. Yaffey, *op. cit.,* p. 46.
27. *Ibid.,* p. 23.
28. Sir Charles Eliot, *The East African Protectorate,* (1905) quoted in Yaffey, p. 43.
29. *Report of the East Africa Commission, op. cit.,* (London, H.M.S.O., 1925).
30. V.I. Lenin, 'Report on the International Situation to the Second Congress of the Communist International, 20 July 1920, *Collected Works,* Vol. 20 (Moscow, Progress).
31. K. Ingham, 'Tanganyika, the Mandate and Cameron 1919-31' in Harlow, Chilvers and Smith, *op. cit.,* p. 545; see also K. Ingham, *A History of East Africa* (London, Longmans, 1966), pp. 292-3.
32. The text of the Mandate is reproduced as an Appendix, Harlow, Chilver and Smith, *op. cit.,* pp. 690-5.
33. Ingham, 'Tanzania, the Mandate', *op. cit.,* p. 548.
34. See Charles Dundas, *A History of German East Africa* (DSM, Government Printer, 1923).
35. Yaffey, *op. cit.,* p. 49.
36. Tanganyika Territory, *Report of the Central Development Committee* (Dar es Salaam, Government Printer, 1940), p. 10.
37. *Ibid.*
38. See K. Ingham, 'Tanganyika: Slump and Short-term Governors 1932-45' in Harlow, Chilver and Smith, *op. cit.,* pp. 606-7.
39. Rappard, 'The Practical Working of the Mandate System', League of Nations, 1926', quoted in Yaffey, *op. cit.,* p. 52.
40. Legislative Council, 7 December 1926, quoted in Yaffey, *op. cit.,* p. 53.
41. Yaffey, *op. cit.,* pp. 53, 62.
42. Tanganyika Territory, *op. cit.,* p. 11.
43. B.R. Fuggles-Couchman, *Agricultural Change in Tanganyika: 1945-1960.*
44. E.A. Brett, *Colonialism and Underdevelopment in East Africa* (London, Heinemann, 1973), pp. 129-38, Stanford, 1964 p. 18.
45. Rodney, *op. cit.,* p. 19.
46. Ingham, 'Tanganyika: Slump', *op. cit.,* pp. 594-5.
47. Tanganyika Territory, *op. cit.,* pp. 10-11.
48. J. Iliffè, *Agricultural Change in Tanganyika* (Nairobi, East Africa Publishing House, 1971), p. 28.
49. Rodney, *op. cit.,* p. 24; Iliffe, *Agricultural Change, op. cit.,* p. 29.
50. Fuggles-Couchman, *op. cit.,* p. 19.
51. Iliffe, *Agricultural Change, op. cit.,* p. 30.
52. Brett, *op. cit.,* p. 138.
53. Tanganyika Territory, *op. cit.,* p. 183.
54. Iliffe, *Agricultural Change, op. cit.,* p. 35.
55. H.H. Beinhammer, 'Institutional Arrangements for Supplying Credit and Finance to the Rural Sector of the Economy of Tanzania', E.R.B. Paper 68. (Dar es Salaam University, 1968), p. 3.
56. Fuggles-Couchman, *op. cit.*
57. Fuggles-Couchman, *op. cit.,* pp. 28-9.
58. C. Leubuscher, *Bulk Buying from the Colonies: A Study of the Bulk Purchase of the Colonial Commodities by the U.K. Government*

(London, Oxford University Press, 1956), p. 142.
59. *Ibid.*, p. 7.
60. *Ibid.*, p. 92.
61. Yaffey, *Balance of Payments, op. cit.*, pp. 64–5.
62. *Ibid.*, p. 65.
63. *Ibid.*, p. 65.
64. Quoted in Brett, *op. cit.*, pp. 273–4.
65. *Ibid.*, p. 268.
66. *Ibid.*, p. 270.
67. I.B.B.D., *The Economic Development of Tanganyika* (Baltimore, Johns Hopkins Press, 1961), pp. 229–32.

3. The Ugandan Colonial Economy

Founding a Colony

The development of the Ugandan colonial economy served the interests of British imperialism in a special way — indeed it would almost appear that the whole colonization of Kenya was conceived as a mere supplement to the exploitation of Uganda. The first major project on which British imperialism was prepared to invest its capital was the Uganda Railway, supposedly for strategic or diplomatic reasons. However, such explanations are superficial and cannot give a scientific understanding of the problem, even in the hands of neo-Marxists.[1] And indeed, the representatives of capitalism could themselves be quite specific as to their real motive. Speaking on behalf of British monopoly capital in a Parliamentary Committee, the Under-Secretary of State for Foreign Affairs as far back as 1895 was quite clear, whatever else was said, about the real aim of the railway:

> The name 'Uganda Railway' suggests the truth as to the principal object of the railway, viz. that is to bring down to the coast the resources not only of the Ganda Protectorate, but of all those countries in the upper waters of the Nile and of the Congo, which surround at no great distance the Victoria Nyanza — resources for which the railway will be the natural outlet.[2]

These areas had been brought under the control of the British imperialists by the colonizing activities of the Imperial British East Africa Company, led by Mackinnon. His own local representative, Lugard, had intervened on behalf of one of the ruling-class factions in Buganda (at the famous Battle of the Mengo) to settle which local faction would act as the agency for British rule. Once a 'mopping-up operation' had been completed, followed by a 'rounding up of rebels' and the establishment of a colonial state structure, the conditions had been laid for creating a proper colonial economy. Rationalized by the colonial bureaucracy as a means of 'raising revenue', in reality it was to be a colonial economy that would allow the full exploitation of the country. This exploitation was rendered easier in those areas of the country where surviving feudal forms made it obligatory for the peasantry to produce a surplus for the nobles. In Buganda, where the victorious *Ingleza* faction had taken upon itself the compradorial role of 'indirect rule' on behalf of the British financial oligarchy, this was particularly pronounced. To facilitate the task, the so-called Uganda Agreement was drawn up under which 50% of the land of Buganda was summarily removed from clan owner- ship and transferred to the British state, while the other half was handed over to the governing faction and various others, including the Kabaka. It was not until 1927, after a long struggle, that the peasants gained any rights of occupancy and this advance can be largely attributed to the fact that the developing form of the colonial economy made the comprador clique less important. At the same time, this move enabled the monopolies to have direct access to low-cost peasant labour, which the comprador landlords were already exploiting.

As well as actual coercion, the Hut and Poll Tax was used as an instru- ment for disciplining the peasants and levelling the conditions of production throughout the country, organizing all the hitherto self-sufficient societies to produce for British industries and markets. The Church, too, was an active agent on behalf of imperialist economic domination; indeed, the Church initiated the first stages of economic exploitation with its experimen- tal introduction of cotton seed. And it was the Church which set up a com- pany with the objective of introducing the African population to industry and 'legitimate trade'.

Cotton, Coffee and Rubber

Fluctuating U.S. cotton prices were having an adverse impact on Britain's textile industry at this time, as they were in Germany. It was thus inevitable that the British textile interests, intervening through the British state, should establish and strengthen their own sources. The formation of the British Cotton Growing Association (B.C.G.A.), with a founding capital of £500,000 was clearly worth the effort,[3] even though the initial plans for large cotton plantations were later given up in favour of smallholding peasant plantations.[4] The supply of cotton seed was itself to become a very important capital investment, changing the conditions of production and mode of calculation of the peasant population. But other factors were involved: the establish- ment of rail transport, buying stations, ginning and baling factories, and advance funds for financing and handling the crop.[5] Thus, cotton growing was to benefit not only the textile interests, but also the iron and steel manufacturing interests, the banks, the merchants and other small British businesses servicing the big monopolies, as well as the colonial bureaucracy and the clergy who were to take a share of the surplus value produced by the peasants.

All these interests thus converged in Uganda in 1903 with the introduction of cotton growing. The B.C.G.A. supplied the Church with the cotton seed. The colonial state joined in by importing 1½ tons of three different types of seed the following year. The seed was distributed to the chiefs in Buganda, Busoga and Bunyoro 'for trial cultivation by peasants in all likely and accessible parts of protectorate'. By 1910 the crop was well established and exports had risen from 241 bales valued at £1,089 in 1905-06 to 13,378 bales valued at £165,412 in 1910-11. As a result government revenue rose from £60,000 in 1904-05 to £191,000 in 1910-11, 'by which time it was in sight of financial self-sufficiency'.[6] This quick result not only impressed the colonial bureaucrats, who looked at the matter from the narrow standpoint of revenue but, more importantly, the monopolists, who were able to boast, 'We are creating an absolutely new trade and [have] enabled the natives to produce an article for export in those districts where an export trade was previously impossible', having noted that, in the countries where the B.C.G.A. was operating, government revenues from the colonies had risen to £130,000 by 1915, and that the shipping and the insurance companies as well as the bankers 'had also benefited'.[7]

Major Leget of the Empire Cotton-Growing Corporation, associated with the B.C.G.A., noted in 1915 that the 15 million people of East Africa, Uganda, the Eastern Congo and the German Lake districts, 'for whom the port of Mombasa is their shortest route to the outside world', were already purchasing 'about eightpence of clothing per annum per head', and that in the more 'forward' regions the figure per head was as high as three to four shillings per annum.[8] Thus, he added, a market was developing alongside production and even at that level of 'civilization' there was thus 'within assured view a jump in the trade of those countries from the five million of last year to something like twenty millions sterling . . . ten million pounds worth of food and raw materials to come each year to the people of Europe and ten million pounds worth of home manufactures to go out in exchange'.[9]

By the time of the 1929-31 Depression, when in settler areas production was stagnating, in Uganda it was increasing; despite fluctuating prices, the colonial state was able to tax an increasing share of the peasants' earnings — over and above the revenue it was already accumulating — as 'price assistance funds' to 'offset inflation'! In 1915-16 the now unnecessary grants-in-aid from the Colonial Office ceased and, as Knowles put it, 'within twenty years a savage country became financially self-supporting'[10] — as if before colonialism it had not been self-supporting!

Cotton was soon supplemented by coffee and rubber. But efforts by white settlers to establish themselves in the field failed completely as African peasants were able to grow coffee at a much cheaper cost. A rubber plantation set up in 1907 by large planters collapsed in 1916 after a difficult period. By 1914 African-grown coffee, both arabica and robusta, earned £23,000 in exports, while settler rubber earned only £3,000. Even then, there were about 1,000 acres of white-planted coffee in Uganda, at a time when very few planters in Kenya had as many as 100. Arabica coffee was first tried out in Mount Elgon in 1912 among the Bagisu peasants, and later among the Bamba in the West, both successful ventures. Thus, here too, while settler coffee in Kenya was in difficulty, Ugandan peasant-produced coffee was 'comparatively buoyant', proving to the financial oligarchy the value of a form of production in which costs were passed on to the peasant

41

families.

As one colonial economist has remarked of coffee growing in Uganda:

> Yet there was no real reason why coffee — arabica in Bugisu, robusta
> elsewhere — should not prosper under African management. The amount
> of skill and care necessary to its survival was relatively small, and in the
> case of robusta practically nil. The argument that Africans could not
> or would not wait for a crop which took three years to mature had
> little force in Buganda. They were able to wait, because their need for
> cash was not pressing . . . . The argument that cultivation had to be
> associated with processing plant that required a large cash outlay was
> equally untenable, for coffee could, though not without some loss
> of quality, be prepared either by the growers with the aid of very
> simple appliances or in central factories run on the same lines as cotton
> ginneries. There could be no doubt that capital and European manage-
> ment made for higher yields and better quality. But the question was
> whether the value added by these factors exceeded their cost; and in
> 1922 the answer appeared to be that it fairly did not. Thus if coffee
> production were to expand at all it would have to do so without their
> aid.[11]

Thus, by 1929 Uganda had fully established itself as a 'prosperous' peasant
economy, cheap and profitable and, further, one which could effectively
subsidize the more costly Kenyan settler agriculture through periods of
crisis by means of the regional horizontal integrative mechanisms to be
discussed in Volume Two. It was also the reason for Uganda's apparent
buoyancy and resilience in agricultural production during the Depression and
the rationale behind the policies of 'paramountcy of African interests' and
the dual economy as finishing touches to colonial policy in East Africa. That
this resilience was due specifically to peasant agriculture as against the small
settler sector in this period was noted by one colonial economist: 'Uganda's
experience of the 1930s was happier than that of countries dependent upon
plantations for their income. Her small plantation sector was sharply affected
by falling prices — the area under non-native coffee fell from approximately
20,000 acres in 1929 to 13,000 acres in 1938. Peasant production was
comparatively buoyant.'[12]

Thus, despite the ups and downs in coffee and cotton production, they
continued to be the major prize of British imperialism in the Empire, making
Uganda a major producer amongst commonwealth countries as late as the
1950s, when, together, coffee and cotton accounted for over two-thirds of
all export earnings of the country. All the cotton exports went to British
manufacturers in the U.K. or India, whence they were sold to other parts
of the world.

That exports should be matched by imports, and hence effect a bilateral
integration of Uganda to the British imperialist economy, was assured through
trade by big merchant houses based either in Kenya or operating from within

Uganda. Together with the banks and insurance houses, these constituted the real links in the chain of British finance capital. In Uganda large monopolies like Ralli Brothers, already mentioned in connection with Tanganyika, were also active in the cotton trade, insurance and shipping, while Dalgety, Smith Mackenzie, the United Africa Company and The Uganda Company all played their part in the activities that tied Uganda's economy to the British metropole. Since major banks, finance houses and insurance companies also operated elsewhere in East Africa, economies of scale encouraged the horizontal integration of the three territories, to the advantage of greater super-profit.

The *exporting* monopolies and banks were themselves dominant in the *import* activities of the colony, smoothing the synchronization of the Ugandan market to the export needs of the British monopolies and siphoning incomes from agricultural production back to the British monopolies. Through exclusive trade agencies and the various mechanisms of tapping 'abnormal incomes' surplus could be extracted all the way along the line.

Here too, as in Tanganyika, the Asian trader was the intermediary between producers and monopoly buyers. Facilitated by finance capital's 'forward funds' through the 90-day credit facility chain (described by one Fabian socialist as 'incredible'), the Asian traders bought in bulk from Europe, sold to retailers who then passed on the manufactured goods to the shops in towns and villages,[13] and also bought from the peasant using the same credit mechanism. In this way, banks got their share of the surplus value from production on both sides.

At first the cotton crop was hand-ginned by the chiefs or producers and bought by the itinerant trader, who sold it to the big trader for shipping. Later this method gave way to a more integrated system where buying centres were set up and gazetted. In these centres cotton and coffee could be sold and ginned, baled and transported to the railhead, and then shipped. This is how the railway not only paid its way but subsidized the more expensive Kenya settler capitalist farmer agriculture; the same holds true for the insurance and shipping monopolies.

Post-War Integration

During the Second World War Ugandan cotton and coffee like Tanganyikan products came under bulk-purchasing contracts by which all the Ugandan coffee was bought by the British Ministry of Food and the India Office. It was also during the war that it became cheaper to ship cotton to Liverpool and onwards through Bombay.[14] Later still, the bulk-purchasing system gave way to the Marketing Board system for both cotton and coffee, in which a parastal bought on the basis of forward prices, and was financed by the banks until the crop was sold overseas.[15] The peasant was then paid a 'final' instalment when the crop was actually being consumed, and was thus in a real way advancing the monopolies' raw materials, not to mention labour power.

The later struggle of the peasants compelled the British Government to allow them co-operative marketing of the crops, a move in which the rich peasant and capitalist farmer played a significant role.[16]

The bulk-purchasing contract not only helped to integrate East African production to the needs of British finance capital, as we have noted with Tanganyika, but also helped to protect the value of sterling by enabling the judicious use of foreign currency. Second, the system ensured that supplies were withheld from the enemy, as well as enabling 'the most efficient use of shipping' during a period of crisis when most ships were requisitioned for use in the war. Third, the system helped eliminate competition 'between British buyers abroad' and, finally, enabled the geographical division of sources of supplies between the consumers of Britain, France, the U.S. and the other Allies.[17] (Later this system of marketing was replaced by the Coffee and Lint Marketing Boards to the advantage of Britain.) But most of all it allowed the Ugandan colonial government to retain a large part of the earnings of the peasants from 1940 onwards in the form of the 'price stabilization fund', amounting to some £10,550,000 by 1948,[18] This money was never repaid to the peasants. Instead, after most of it was distributed to development projects, in 1949 £3,925,000 was put straight into another 'price assistance fund'. This fund accumulated to such an extent that by 1952–53, there was amassed, as the East African Royal Commission noted, £44,475,000, or nearly £9,000,000 per annum, 'a sum equal to the total African wage bill of Uganda in 1952 or 23% of the total African income that year'.[19]

This was quite apart from the state-imposed taxes on those crops which accounted for 16% of earnings by 1945, and 52% by 1952.[20] Between 1945 and 1960 cotton growers paid 32% of their income in tax, 18% to 'development projects', and 12% in 'price assistance funds' – altogether £83.7 million. Likewise, coffee growers paid 26.5% of their income in tax, totalling £35.3 million between the same dates.[21] Between 1945 and 1960, therefore, the state recapitalized altogether £119.0 million, or about 51.3% of the total earnings on the two crops.

This colossal exploitation of the peasantry had been made possible by the mechanisms of regional integration and it was this regional integration which was now under strain. Reaching the limits of taxation in this way, the colonial state turned to other means of extracting income which tended to produce conflict with Kenya over revenue sources, as Table 2 illustrates. It shows that for the years 1945–60 cotton-producing peasants received only 38.1% of the total price of the crop, while the state took, in various forms, a total of 61.9% of the receipts; the coffee-producing peasants received 63.5% as against 36.5% appropriated by the colonial state in various ways. Taken together, the peasant producers of both coffee and cotton received 48.7% of their product, against the state's share of 51.3%.

Shifting Class Formations
By 1945 these developments had produced class differentiations in the countryside, particularly in Buganda and other kingdom areas where class

Table 2
Distribution of Export Income from Coffee and Cotton in Uganda, 1945-60

	Cotton		*Coffee*		*Cotton and Coffee*	
	Millions £	*%*	*Millions £*	*%*	*Millions £*	*%*
Contribution to Development Funds	24.2	17.9	0.6	0.6	24.8	10.7
Export taxes a) for development budget	12.3	9.1	7.0	7.2	19.3	8.3
b) for current budget	31.2	23.1	17.7	18.3	48.9	21.1
Increase in price assistance funds	13.9	10.3	8.9	9.2	22.8	9.8
Depreciation (net)	2.0	1.5	1.1	1.2	3.2	1.4
Payment to growers	51.6	38.1	61.3	63.5	112.9	48.7
Total receipts	*135.3*	*100.0*	*96.6*	*100.0*	*231.9*	*100.0*

Source: D.A. Lury, *East Africa Economic Review*, Vol. 10, No. 1, 1963, p. 52.

societies had already emerged in pre-colonial Uganda. The 1927 Busulu and Envujjo Law in Buganda had enabled capitalist farming in relatively small peasant holdings to compete successfully with the large landlord holdings as well as the large capitalist farms. By the 1950s this differentiation had become sufficiently pronounced, as in Tanganyika, to justify the colonial governments' preference for the rich peasant or 'progressive farmer'. The 'ignorant man with a hoe', that is, the poor and middle peasant, was now looked down upon compared with the rich farmer who would utilize tractors and fertilizers.[22]

This change in policy coincided with, or rather was partly the result of, the on-going anti-colonial struggle in which the rich peasant was playing a vocal and leading role, resulting in the 1945 and 1949 'disturbances' in Uganda. Clearly there was need to take advantage of this force and cut it off from the mass of the poor peasantry who, together with the workers, constituted the greater threat to colonialism. This interest was compounded by British colonialism's need to improve productivity on the land and increase exports to earn dollars to repay debts incurred to the U.S. during the Second World War.

It is for this reason that the East African Royal Commission was appointed to enquire into problems of land use, and particularly the best way in which agricultural development could be encouraged through enlarged credit for the 'progressive' farmer. As a result of the 1949 peasant riots in Buganda, the Kingdon Commission had recommended the urgent setting up of a credit or land bank, 'lest through delay and disappointment another grievance arises'.[23] In 1950 the Uganda Credit and Savings Bank was created on the basis of the peasants' own earnings to give loans to the rich peasantry. U.S.-financed loans were also made available for the same purpose.[24] Developments in scientific research for agricultural production gave further impetus to agricultural growth — with most of this research funded out of peasants' earnings taxed for 'development purposes'.

With these measures land productivity improved considerably, despite the fact that Uganda received very little of the Colonial Welfare and Development funds.[25] As a result of what was effectively peasant self-financed exploitation, 'a wholly new system of seed replacement' for cotton and coffee was designed and implemented during these years. Consequently, the parity to variety in Bugandan cotton was raised from 75 to 90% and the average ginning outrun between 1945 and 1960 rose from 30 to 33%.[26] Between 1947 and 1950 the value of exports increased by nearly 150%, between 1950 and 1952 by another 65%, and the geographical income increased by 46%.[27] These increases were partly due to the money value adjustments related to the devaluation of the British pound, but principally reflected improved production techniques.

But all these developments were facilitated by the granting of credits to the capitalist farmer and rich peasant in Buganda and to a lesser extent to rich peasants in other parts of the country. It was the Uganda Credit and Savings Bank, established after the riots in 1949 with a capital of £600,000 out of the peasants' own enforced savings, which was the enabling condition. By 1953, 1,285 loans had been granted, half of which went to agriculture. In 1950 loans worth Shs. 829,300 were disbursed, of which Shs. 214,300 went to agriculture. Further loan schemes were created to extend credit to these farmers. An African Loans Fund operated outside Buganda where no land security existed. In 1956–57 Shs. 1,017,200 were granted to 358 applicants, mainly for agricultural improvement. Another U.S.-sponsored Revolving Fund, as well as a Progressive Farmers Loans Scheme, was established to develop agriculture further for export to Britain and to dollar areas in order to earn Britain hard currency.

The pressure from British finance capital to improve productivity was the result, as we have already observed, of the widening crisis in the British competitive position in an increasingly American-dominated world market. All imperial efforts were directed at saving Britain's dollar reserves and all the colonies were instructed to increase production and direct these products to areas where dollars and gold could be earned.

Production to earn hard currency for Britain also implied a reduction in consumption of goods by the colonies from non-sterling areas. In Uganda the consumption of petrol, rubber and cotton piecegoods was curtailed, and a Piecegoods Buying Pool was formed for the purpose of distributing the limited supplies.[28] The restrictions were mainly directed against Japan and it was in this atmosphere that textile manufacturing in Uganda was encouraged as part of the defence against Japanese competition. Indeed, most of the industrialization permitted in this period was in relation to the curtailment of supplies of consumer goods.

The construction of the Nile hydro-electric plant at Jinja was the beginning of the extension of manufacturing beyond cotton and coffee processing. With the exception of a tobacco factory, which had been allowed to operate only because the Ugandan Government had undertaken to purchase the tobacco crop not required by the British American Tobacco Company, no other major industry had hitherto existed. Here again, British finance capital had access to the funds accumulated under the cotton and coffee 'price assistance' funds of the peasants to invest in industrial activities through the state monopoly, the Uganda Development Corporation.

Large amounts of money were invested in construction and public works. In 1951 alone, £1,886,000 was invested in new buildings and roads, as compared to £364,000 in 1947.[29] These works, in particular the hydro-electric project, necessitated in turn the construction of a cement factory. Within a short time the Uganda Development Corporation, which started with a capital of Shs. 5 million from peasant savings, was in a position to establish — in partnership with British, foreign and local finance capital — a number of enterprises, and by 1956 jointly operated cement, textile, metal, chemical and fertilizer plants, which in turn generated secondary enterprises.

By 1957 the number of enterprises listed and operating under the Factories Ordinance of 1952 was 1,176.[30] Local Asian-owned enterprises also began to blossom, with investments in oil mills, soap factories and confectionery and can-making factories, as well as breweries. All these investments went to save Britain's expenditure of dollars and other foreign currency, as well as enabling a level of import substitution, and hence savings, on transport costs for certain bulky products.

Thus, as we approach the end of the period of British colonialism in Uganda, the economy was very much a reflection of the history of the British imperialist economy. But the exploitation of the people by the British imperialists had met with increasing resistance. Beginning in the late 1930s, new types of organizations representing traders, peasants, workers and intellectuals, were emerging to demand an end to the oppressive system. The formation of the Uganda Motor Drivers' Association in 1938 — the first workers' organization — inspired the peasants' own *Bana ba Kintu* movement. Later, in 1946, both these organizations converged as a political movement under the Bataka Party, which led the 1949 riots. Despite efforts by British imperialism at reform, the struggle for national independence never relented.

References

1. See also E.A. Brett, *Colonialism and Underdevelopment in East Africa: The Politics of Economic Change 1919–39* (London, Heinemann, 1973), pp. 80, 200.
2. Quoted in M.F. Hill, *The Permanent Way: The Story of the Kenya and Uganda Railway* (Nairobi, East African Railways and Harbours, 1961), p. 131.
3. L.C.A. Knowles, *The Economic Development of the British Overseas Empire*, (London, George Routledge and Sons, 1924), p. 132.
4. *Ibid.*, p. 132.
5. *Ibid.*
6. C.C. Wrigley, *Crops and Wealth in Uganda* (London, Oxford University Press, 1970), p. 15.
7. Knowles, *op. cit.*
8. *Ibid.*, p. 105.
9. *Ibid.*, p. 506.
10. *Ibid.*
11. Wrigley, p. 40.
12. C.C. Erlich, 'The Uganda Economy 1903–45' in Harlow, Chilvers and Smith (eds.), *History of East Africa* (London, Oxford University Press, 1965), p. 457.
13. J. Stonehouse, *Prohibited Immigrant* (London, Faber, 1960), p. 91; see also M. Mamdani, *Politics and Class Formation in Uganda* (London, Heinemann, 1975), p. 168.
14. C. Leubuscher, *Bulk Buying from the Colonies*, (London, Oxford University Press, 1956), pp. 29–41.
15. *Ibid.*, pp. 55–66.
16. D.W. Nabudere, *Imperialism and Revolution in Uganda* (London/Dar es Salaam, Onyx/Tanzania Publishing House, 1980), pp. 89–94.
17. Leubuscher, *op. cit.*, p. 2.
18. H.M.S.O./Hansard, Parliamentary Debates, House of Commons, Vol. 456, 8–19 December, 1948, pp. 1–4.
19. H.M.S.O. Cmnd. 9253, *The Royal East African Report, 1952–53.*
20. R. van Zwanenberg and A. King, *An Economic History of Kenya and Uganda, 1800–1970* (Nairobi, East Africa Publishing House, 1975), p. 220.
21. *Ibid.*
22. C.C. Wrigley, 'African Farming in Buganda', mimeo, E.A.I.S.R. Conference Papers (Kampala, 1953), section 9.
23. Uganda Protectorate, *Report of the Commission of Inquiry into Disturbances in Uganda during April 1949* (Entebbe, Government Printer, 1949), pp. 95, 119.
24. D. Hunt, *Credit for Agricultural Development: A Case Study of Uganda* (Nairobi, East Africa Publishing House, 1975).
25. C.B. Masefield, *Agricultural Change in Uganda, 1945–60* (Stanford, Food Research Institute, 1962), pp. 100–1.
26. *Ibid.*, p. 101.
27. Lord Hailey, *An African Survey* (1956) (Rev's ed.), p. 1298.
28. Mamdani, *op. cit.*, p. 251.

29. Hailey, *op. cit.*, p. 1298.
30. W. Elkans, *The Economic Development of Uganda* (London, Oxford University Press, 1961), pp. 5–6.

4. The Kenyan Colonial Economy

The territory now known as Kenya was created out of the smaller East African Protectorate, which covered the coastal area and some undefined interior up to Uganda. In 1902 it was widened by bringing within its orbit most of the fertile highlands west of the Rift Valley, previously part of the Eastern Province of Uganda.[1] The colonization of Kenya was therefore part and parcel of the acquisition of Uganda. Indeed it was seen as a means of protecting communications between Uganda and the coast, Kenya itself being considered a 'barren wilderness' which 'hampered' the vital links with Uganda.[2] Thus, the creation of Kenya, which ultimately came to be an area of white settlement, and the problem it posed for colonial policy must be analysed in the context of how the colonialists conceived of the overall situation in the territory.

Land and Legitimation

The fact that there was no articulated class rule in Kenya, and therefore no existing ruling class with whom alliances could be struck in order to sub-jugate the area, is a central circumstance. The way in which the absence of class rule in Kenya was used as a cover for the actions of the colonialists provides an example of the ingenuity of imperialist ideology and the real effects which such efforts at legitimization could have. Rosa Luxembourg pointed out[3] that where land did not belong to a sovereign, the imperialists would invariably attribute the ownership of such lands to some existing sovereign and then coerce the sovereign to surrender the land to them!
In the case of Kenya no such sovereign existed, so, it was argued, a different form of 'legal' argumentation was required. In order to resolve the 'legal doubts' that existed over the acquisition of crown lands and encourage the settlement of white farmers in Kenya, the legal officers of the Crown had to distinguish first between those countries where a 'foreign sovereign' existed and those where 'partial sovereignty' acquired from the sovereign did not give the imperialists any 'title to the soil'. In the latter case, the land would be 'foreign soil' and could not vest in Her Majesty, 'as in the case of territory which is actually annexed to the British dominions'. But, as was the case

with Kenya, 'where there are no such owners, and the land can be regarded as vacant, the object desired may be attained by other methods'.

The legal officers then argued that in such a case British authorities could, by administrative action alone, permit a person to take possession of land, subject to the conditions attached by the authorities to such possession. With respect to Kenya it was claimed that any sovereignty which could be said to exist was held by 'small chiefs or elders' who, for all practical purposes, were 'savages', particularly as 'the idea of tribal ownership in the land is unknown'. Thus, the existence of a Protectorate in such an 'uncivilized country' implied the right to assume 'whatever jurisdiction, over all persons for the proper exercise of the Protectorate'.[4]

It was on the basis of such tortuous argument that the Governor was held to be capable of granting land to settlers by administrative action alone, without any need to refer to the Foreign or Colonial Office at home. Under these legalized administrative powers, not only over land considered 'vacant' but also over all 'persons', the Governor was able to dispossess the African people of their lands and grant leases to alien settlers at a rental of 15 rupees for 100 acres for a period of 99 years. Actual sale of land at 2 rupees per acre was also carried out, even before the passage of the law. The ease with which this robbery took place and the administrative autonomy which was granted to the colonial officers typified British imperialism's callous intervention in the political economy of Kenya.

All these manoeuvres were connected with the whole question of how Kenya was to be turned into a productive colony for British finance capital, and by whom. To the extent that decisions were made by on-the-spot representatives of the financial oligarchy, state officials were relatively free agents. Already in 1893 before Kenya was declared a Protectorate, Lord Lugard, in his capacity as agent of the Imperial British East Africa Company, had observed that this part of East Africa, particularly the part around Mau escarpment, was the best place for white settlement. He had pointed out that the area was 'uninhabited' and therefore offered 'unlimited room for the location of agricultural settlements or stock-raising farms'. Here, if anywhere in Central Africa, 'would be the site upon which to attempt the experiment of European settlements' for a 'fruit export' of the kind which had proved successful in New Zealand and California.[5]

Of the officials responsible for laying the foundation of what was to be a special type of settlement policy in East Africa, Charles Eliot was particularly influential. He had been moved from Zanzibar in 1900 to be the first Commissioner in what came to be known as Kenya. In his first report to London he observed that the famine of 1897 had left the Kikuyu population disorganized. Agricultural production had collapsed, leaving them wholly dependent on 'warfare' for their livelihood. Elsewhere, among the Kavirondo and other groups around Lake Victoria, some agriculture was in evidence, but it was unreliable because of the local population's indulgence in alcohol and leisure, 'a major barrier to sustained productive activity'. The nomadic Masai, he continued, were 'utterly non-productive' and should not be allowed to roam over areas they would not easily cultivate. Kenya was contrasted with the orderly production found in neighbouring Uganda.

The Settlement Question

To the bureaucrat whose job was to make the colony pay for its 'keep' as quickly as possible, the solution for the country lay in white settlement. As one white settler was later to record, 'The British Government had built 580 expensive miles of line, and now every train that ran along it did so at heavy loss. Somehow or other the railway had got to be made to pay . . . . The British taxpayer could not go on making good the deficit for ever.'[6] Since the country through which the 580 miles of track ran was 'economically dead country', what was required was 'development', and since the Africans could not, 'within a measurable distance of time, produce enough surplus goods to feed the railway', the only hope lay with settlers, who could 'fill up these empty, dead spaces along the line', turn the country, the fertile but now wasted soil, 'to useful account', grow crops for the railway to carry out and buy machinery and other goods for it to carry in.[7]

> Settlers must somehow be found, attracted, encouraged, started off. There was no other alternative but economic stagnation and a perpetual bleeding of the British Treasury. East Africa could be transformed from a liability into an asset only if the government could succeed in getting a thriving white population established to add to the wealth that the world still wanted and was prepared to pay for; to feed the railway; to buy goods from Britain's factories; to provide the outlet of employment for the surplus energies of idle young tribesmen whose only occupations of raiding and fighting were being barred to them by the spread of law and order; to start the wheels of trade by employing natives and so circulating among them money with which they could buy imported goods and pay hut tax; to bring capital into the country; to pay taxes; to improve useless land by watering, draining, grazing, cultivating; to give permanence and stability to British rule in East Africa — in short, to build by their efforts a self-supporting colony.[8]

This ideology became the very basis for framing the policy of the British financial oligarchy in relation to the colony. Despite the racial twist in the above argument, it was clear that what finance capital wanted was to turn the area to production not for the sake of Kenya, not for the well-being of the native population as such, nor for that matter for that of the white settlers as such, but for the reproduction of British finance capital and the wealth of the parasitic imperialist bourgeoisie which, though nowhere to be seen on the spot, was acting through its agencies.

However, as far as the imperialist bourgeoisie were concerned, white settlement was not a foregone conclusion. Indeed the initial British official position, as formulated by the Foreign Office to the Kenya Commissioner, was to *discourage* such settlement. As far back as 1885 the British Imperial

East Africa Company in its Charter had clearly expressed preference for the 'colonization' of the territory by natives of the Indian subcontinent. Officials in the Foreign Office also argued in favour of Indians undertaking the economic management of East Africa. East Africa was seen as playing a role analogous to that of America in the Atlantic.[9]

It was in this context that Eliot, reacting to the 'mounting pressure' for concrete steps towards economic development, permitted the immigration of Indian agricultural settlers.[10] Sir Clement Hill, head of the Africa Department in the Foreign Office, approvingly seconded the efforts in this direction: 'We are looking to India for our East African system and for development'.[11] In pursuit of this policy, in 1902 Eliot issued free grants of land, free seed and agricultural loans to Indian settlers in the Highlands.[12] But in 1906 an official mission sent to the Punjab to recruit Indian families for settlement found that the potential settlers were interested in immigration only if 'whole Indian villages' could move together, 'a course London deemed to be expensive'.[13] One economist has observed, 'The mass movement of a poor peasantry, especially under the stringent conditions on which the Government of India insisted, would have required organization and finance on a scale far beyond the resources of the early protectorate'.[14]

Joseph Chamberlain visited East Africa himself in 1902 and even suggested that the Jewish refugees from Poland and Russia should take up the territory, but the Zionist Congress rejected the so-called 'Uganda Offer' in 1905. Still, the idea of non-British immigration was not abandoned and the Foreign Office went on to suggest to Eliot that Finns be settled in the Highlands. But Eliot, who had 'knowledge of Finland' — acquired during his service at the Embassy of St. Petersburg — advised against the idea which was then abandoned.[15]

In the meantime, a number of private individuals and enterprises in Britain were exploring the possibilities of settlement and production in Kenya. In this effort they found a sympathetic supporter in Commissioner Eliot who, after 1901, had come round to the idea of British rather than Indian settlers. By this time there were a few dozen European settlers in the territory, who in 1902 founded a Society to Promote European Immigration and exclude Indian settlers who, with lower incomes, lower profits and a closely knit community organization, would have offered stiff competition, both in agriculture and commerce. It was these European settlers who in 1901 appealed to Eliot to end the official policy of sponsoring Indian immigration, and, indeed, with the failure of the other efforts, Eliot was now given a free hand to encourage white settlement, initially by sending a recruitment mission to South Africa. By 1912 the South African white settlers outnumbered immigrants from Britain.

Having at last settled the question, the colonial administration began the alienation of land to white capitalist farmers. We have seen how Eliot moved to do this without actually waiting for any instructions from the Foreign Office (as was required by the Order in Council of 1901). His subsequent actions on land acquisition were equally characterized by 'illegality', yet there were no protests as they did not contradict finance capital's interest in getting the colony on its feet.

Whereas the Crown Lands Ordinance of 1902, originating in the British Foreign Office, clearly laid down the conditions for carrying out settlement — sales to a single applicant not to exceed 1,000 acres, leases not to exceed 99 years — in practice, these conditions were modified to meet the situation. In order to attract settlers, provisions for covenants to pay rent, restrictions on the transfer of land and interference with native settlements were set aside. Since the Commissioner was empowered to make additional rules under the Ordinance, the guidelines were effectively replaced with what became known as the Homestead Rules. First of all, grants were made on terms more liberal than the Ordinance permitted. Then in 1903 rules were introduced to permit free grants of land in 'less favoured' areas in order to attract more settlers between Mazeras and Machakos Road.

Until 1915 it was these rules rather than the Ordinance which governed the process of land alienation for most of the Highlands. Efforts by the Colonial Office to prevent large-scale speculative landholding (usually arranged by a process known as 'dummying' — applying for extra land in the name of dependents) had also been abandoned. By 1915 the restriction to 99-year leases had given way to the 999 years demanded by the settlers. The result was that the Crown Lands Ordinance of 1915 did little more than 'legalize' the earlier actions of the Governor, consolidating them into a comprehensive law. It did, however, make illegal any land grants to Indian and other non-European capitalists, while not excluding 'Americans'.

African peasants' rights to land were legally restricted to occupation, cultivation and grazing. No other title was recognized. Even areas in Laikipia recognized by 'law' as being native by 'a special treaty' with the Masai, under which they had allegedly 'agreed' of their own 'free will' to be removed to 'definite and final reserves' for the 'undoubted good of our races', were also appropriated, despite the categoric statement in the Treaty that 'so long as the Masai as a race shall exist, "Europeans" or other settlers' should not be allowed to take up land in this reserve.

Instead, another treaty was forced on them under which they also 'agreed of their own free will' that it was 'in the interest of the tribe [no longer 'race' – *Author*] that the Masai people should inhabit one area' (*sic*!). When this flagrant robbery was later challenged by a section of the Masai in Her Majesty's High Court, it was thrown out on the ground that the courts had no jurisdiction in the matter, and the Appeals Court even refused to hear the case on the ground that it was an 'act of state' and hence out of bounds.

All this legalized robbery of land went hand in hand with the legalized theft of Masai and Nandi cattle. In 1885, 1900, 1902, 1903 and again in 1905 the imperialists mounted punitive raids against the Nandi. The Masai, who in 1904 had probably the greatest wealth in cattle — over 50,000 head — as well as 600,000 sheep and goats, lost most of them in similar raids. The Nandi and Masai cattle were then sold cheap to white capitalist settlers for 'breeding up' at a time when the importation of livestock was 'extremely expensive and risky', and the proceeds were then appropriated by the state as compensation for 'military costs'.[17]

The fact that imperialism respects no law or treaty which was an obstacle to its interests becomes even clearer with the infringement of the Native Lands Trust Ordinance of 1930, within two years of its passage. Gold was found near Kakamega – a densely populated Kavirondo reserve. Despite the Ordinance requirement to provide alternative land where encroachment was considered necessary, the gold-bearing area was simply detached from the reserve without compensation. Gold-mining was seen as offering a chance of employment for white capitalist farmers whose farms were collapsing due to the Depression.

Under these various methods of acquisition, large tracts of land were alienated to individual capitalist farmers and large syndicates of merchants and investors in England at little or no cost. One such syndicate – the East African Syndicate – was allocated 500 square miles by the Foreign Office itself. In the Rift Valley two syndicates and four individuals were given 50% of all the land. These large combines were encouraged and even subsidized to search for minerals and to experiment in the cultivation of crops like rubber and cotton. Individual capitalist farmers were granted the best areas in the Highlands: one such man, Delamere, ultimately accumulated, through 'dummying' and other means, over one million acres for himself.[18]

By 1915, 8,242 square miles (4,500 acres) had been allocated to about 1,000 settler capitalist farmers and syndicates. It was, however, very unevenly distributed, with 20% held by five individuals or groups. By 1934, after the investigation of a land commission, 16,700 square miles of all the land available were reserved for white capitalist settlement (about 20% of all usable land) and only 48,000 square miles had been gazetted for African use – a population of 3¼ million, half of which was crammed into the 8,856 square miles in the Kikuyu and Kavirondo areas.

Yet despite all this concentration of land into white capitalist settlement, most of it was controlled by a very small number for speculative purposes and in 1930, 64.8% of this land was not being used for agricultural purposes. Predictions about European capitalist production had not been fulfilled. The production of wool and wheat had suffered real setbacks by 1910; coffee production was insignificant, and no sisal plantation was as yet in evidence. The flow of capital had almost ceased and the original investors 'were near the end of their resources'.[19] Also, with the hostility to African participation and the pressure for labour for European capitalist farmers the cotton planting which had been introduced in 1904 in the Nyanza Province had failed. Nonetheless, African agriculture in other crops like simsim, groundnuts and maize prospered, an advantage of the 'dual policy' for settlers and Africans that was to be argued later.

By 1910 the European capitalist farmers had also rejected cotton as a possible crop, since the return on it was too low. After 1910 some capital began to flow in again with the arrival of another set of settlers, 'of upper-class and middle-class' origins who 'for the first time could see a way to combine the pleasure of life in East Africa with reasonable prospect of profit'.[20] World prices for coffee and rubber had risen, and hence it was to be coffee production which finally improved the prospects for settler capitalist farmers, combined with all the support measures that the state was to make on their behalf.

Despite these high hopes for settler capitalist farming, it was actually African agriculture that was providing the basis of the export earnings of Kenya — up to 1914 the peasant-grown crops, including maize, accounted for 75% of the value of the colony's exports. Ironically, African agriculture was generating the government revenue increasingly used to help European capitalist agriculture and infrastructure.[21]

This preferential treatment cannot be reduced to an issue of racism. There were many interests involved in the state's agricultural investment bias. Many of the white farmers developed ties with the British companies who sold them machinery, fertilizers, insecticides, etc., sometimes on credit terms. Many trading companies also became agents in handling the produce, not to mention the banks that extended the finances required. These companies and banks were therefore deeply involved in the settler economy and, as a result, had considerable influence in creating pressure both at home and in the colony. And as long as cheap African labour was available, supplemented through the East African inter-territorial horizontal integrative mechanisms by cheap peasant production in Uganda and Tanganyika, this served British imperialism well.

The end of the First World War provided a fresh inflow of settlers under the Soldiers Settlement Scheme. Two hundred and fifty-seven farms of 160 acres each were to be given free, 1,053 farms covering 2,500,000 acres were to be sold for 6s. 8d. to 13s. 4d. (sterling) per acre,[22] and the money required for this scheme was raised in London. Since Kenya had been reduced to the status of a colony, it became easier under the Colonial Stocks Act to raise the necessary £5 million — more than two and a half times the current government revenue — at 6½%, part of which was utilized to pay earlier loans for the settlers.

The intention of this scheme was to double the number of white capitalist farmers by means of these soldiers and officers.[23] A British Government-supported scheme for disabled soldiers to grow flax was also launched with £8,000-£10,000. Secondly, the Economic and Financial Committee set up in 1922 recommended that the soldiers should undertake maize production, a crop for which there was 'a steady and virtually unlimited demand in the markets of the world'. Every assistance was given by the colonial state to enable the success of this project and, not surprisingly, maize production proved a saviour for the less capitalized soldier farmer and other small farmers. Large areas of the Highlands, especially the Rift Valley and the newly settled Trans-nzoia, were devoted entirely to the crop. In other areas coffee, sisal and cattle-raising continued to provide the settler population with profitable occupations.

Crisis and the 'Dual Policy'

A period of crisis for the small capitalist farmer was ushered in with falling prices in 1919 and 1920, coupled with the devaluation, as a result of which many of the newly arrived settlers left, or found their farms mortgaged and so had to turn themselves into workers for large plantations, big farmers or for the railways or the government. Government protection and support enabled some capitalist farmers to stay to face the next crisis in 1929–33. The Tariff Amendment Ordinance of 1923 provided great relief by introducing protective duties on a very wide range of temperate-climate foodstuffs, like wheat flour, butter, cheese, bacon, ham, timber, sugar, ghee, tea and beer, and it is here that the horizontal integration in East Africa proved to be of such value to British interests in Kenya. At the same time, the capitalist farmers' tax burdens were reduced by 'the small print of the tariff',[24] by pushing resources from state revenue in the direction of the farmer.

Specific tariff duties as high as 70% were imposed on non-luxury necessities, such as clothing, consumed by the African peasant, while imports of goods for settler capitalist agriculture carried no more than a 30% tariff. Furthermore, the African Hut and Poll Taxes were raised from Shs. 10 to Shs. 16, at a time when white capitalist farmers paid virtually no tax and were actively demanding that they should not pay any income tax either, (which in any case they managed to defer until 1935). Although the Hut Tax was later reduced to Shs. 12 as a result of resistance led by Harry Thuku's Young Kikuyu Association, it imposed a great strain on peasant agriculture which began to decline.

As has already been pointed out, peasant agriculture in Uganda and Tanganyika was at this time also being taxed by means of the railway freight rates in order to assist settler agriculture in Kenya. The 1922 rates revisions reduced the charges on maize and other Kenyan products, while the charges on Ugandan cotton were raised, together with freight charges on imported textiles consumed by African peasants and others in the three territories. This was basically a way of subsidizing the settler capitalist farmer. The doctrine that 'people who contributed capital and enterprise to the country must not fail'[25] was used as a pretext to exploit the African people, and was finally in the interests of the British imperialists – for the people 'who had invested capital and enterprise' were the banks, merchandizing houses and other financial institutions. It was not for nothing that: 'During the 1920s . . . a number of large firms engaged in Oriental and Australian trade, such as Dalgetys, Mitchell Cotts and Leslie and Anderson, came to regard East Africa as worthy of their attention, so that skilled commercial and financial services were now more readily available to producers.'[26]

While the banks and countless other trading houses had already been on the spot, it is important to realize that all these developments, which on the surface appear to be solely in the interest of the white capitalist farmer, in fact served the interests of British finance capital, which must be regarded as the ultimate exploiter of the people. Thus, the question of keeping settler agriculture afloat was not just a problem of land, railway rates, taxes and loans, but essentially one of dispossessing the African people of their land and cattle, of their forcible recruitment on settler farms as labourers; the problem of the tax was just an aspect of this. The white capitalist farmers could extract their share of the surplus value, but the real benefit went to the big banks and industries back home and elsewhere.

Of course, the whole idea of congesting Africans in 'reserves' was to ensure a labour supply. But the imposition of the Hut and Poll taxes was also connected with the new alternative of working on public works instead of paying cash which implied working for the capitalist settlers. From £3,328 in 1901-02, the revenue from the Hut and Poll levies had risen to £591,424 in 1930, compared to the European settlers' tax contribution in 1926 of £7,500, and £21,000 paid by Asian traders.

The Native Registration Ordinance of 1915 was also intended to recruit labour by introducing the pass system, compounded by the subsequent 'Northey Circulars' that intensified forms of control. Africans were recruited to the Carrier Corps not only for the general purpose of discipline, but also for quite specific tasks — 150,000 of them were commandeered as labourers for the settler capitalist farmers. All this supplemented the squatter system by which the excess population from the overpopulated reserves was siphoned off. By law they were required to work at least 180 days of the year for wages. The law also tried to put a stop to the 'Kaffir' farming that was being carried on by squatters on a very limited scale on some of the settler lands.

With these hostile measures by the colonial state against African peasant production, even the increasing population could not offset the decline in African agriculture. Whereas up to 1914 African agriculture had accounted for 75% of exports, by 1928 it only accounted for 20%, most of it in hides and skins, simsim and maize. Even these were increasingly being taken over by the white capitalist farmers, since it was the 'wish of the government that Africans should go out to work'.[27] Any suggestion that African peasants should grow coffee was opposed by the capitalist farmers, and Africans were prohibited from growing coffee not only in Kenya but in Tanganyika under the Germans as well, where the rationale offered was that African peasant-grown coffee would bring 'disease' to the settlers' coffee fields.

In fact the whole problem was one of competition between the relatively more powerful white capitalist farmer and the peasant who could produce significantly more cheaply. The elimination of the weaker African peasant not only reduced competition but enabled the settler to employ him in periods of labour shortage.

Hostility towards the African peasants was particularly manifest at a meeting of East African settler farmers in 1927 at Tukuyu, where it was agreed to oppose all government help to Africans cultivating 'economic crops' like Arabica coffee, tobacco, and even cotton, because of the alleged 'sloth-fulness' of the male African peasant. In 1925 the East Africa Commission had concluded that the Kenya Government was justified in prohibiting the African peasant from growing Arabica coffee on the grounds that 'the present difficulty in obtaining labour in Uganda . . . is due to the high prices which the Ugandan native is at present obtaining for his cotton crop'.[28]

These sectional interests of the small and relatively large settler farmer (from which imperialism also benefited) did not altogether close down the alternatives in African peasant agriculture, particularly in such periods of crisis as 1919-21 and the Depression, when the State was all too happy to fall back on African production.

Despite all the efforts made to support the white capitalist farmer, it was the large plantation industries that won the day in agriculture. Responsible for some coffee, their real value lay in sisal planting on the coast, to which was added a third crop, tea. After 1925 the tea crop attracted a lot of capital from London and large plantations were set up in the Southwestern Highlands, where rainfall was adequate for its production; by 1938 it was second only to coffee as Kenya's export crop.

At this time, African peasant cotton planting was showing some improvement in Nyanza Province, where production increased from one million lbs. in 1930 to nearly 24 million lbs. in 1937-38. African peasant maize production also improved, filling the gap left by the effect of the Depression on settler production when some 200 farms collapsed. The collapse of primary commodity prices on the world market between 1929 and 1934 had reduced the local value of coffee by more than half, and the value of sisal and maize by more than two-thirds.

The Depression and the Growth of Credit

While the Depression affected all of East Africa, Kenya differed from Uganda and Tanganyika in the heavy extent that finance capital had invested in the settler economy. Hence, British finance capital quickly moved in to protect its investments. In alleviating the debt burden of capitalist farmers, and thus enabling them to carry on production, the financial houses were merely taking steps to ensure that the money sunk into farms would not be lost. Thus the so-called hegemony of the settlers over the territorial economy of Kenya should more properly be seen as the dominance of the particular finance capital interests that supported them.

The first step was taken by the colonial state. When commercial banks would no longer give credit, a loans scheme under the Agricultural Advances Ordinance of 1930 was introduced by which a Central Board was set up to advance credit to the settlers who had 'exhausted existing sources of credit', or to make payments of interest on mortgages or overdrafts and 'prevent foreclosure' by the banks. The gravity of the situation can be gauged from the replies to a questionnaire on farmers' debts sent out by the Central Board in 1933 to 942 farmers. Of these only 559 (the main growers) replied, 412 of whom were producing 75% of the total output of the coffee industry.[29] Their aggregate indebtedness was £1,165,558, in addition to an estimated £272,000 in seasonal loans and shortfalls on advances from the previous year. But this was not the entire debt, which, according to an Agricultural

Indebtedness Committee estimate in 1936, amounted to £3,000,000.

This was large compared with the total public debt of the colony of £17 million in 1930, of which £13 million had been raised by the Uganda Railway and the other £4 million by the Kenya administration. In 1931, the total annual repayment of interest on these loans was taking 33% of the entire recurrent revenue of the colony,[30] an 'inflexible obligation which assumed the proportions of a considerable burden', since revenues were also falling at this time. This not only 'pointed to the direction of the collapse of the economy of Kenya as a viable entity',[31] but to a gigantic loss by finance capital of over £20 million in debts owed. The creation of the Land Bank in 1931, therefore, was a welcome step for the banks.

Barclays Bank and the Standard Bank, which in 1928 had been invited to participate in the creation of this new bank, had resisted getting involved in 'local political controversy', and this was typical of the position of most of the commercial interests at this time.[32] But by 1930 the situation was such that 'the slump in prices left the banks with a large number of unprofitable creditors', leaving them little alternative save 'stopp[ing] loans and encourag-[ing] the Land Bank, which could ensure repayment of their debts'.[33]

Thus, when the Central Board stopped giving loans in 1934 and wound up its activities, the Land Bank took over its function; as Governor Grigg maintained before the Hilton Young Commission in 1931: 'The banking system of Kenya had been carried [*sic*] far beyond the normal range of operations of a commercial bank [and the banks were taking] the view that further financing of farming on the present basis is not within their proper duties.'[34] Thus roughly £1,000,000 in all was handled by the Land Bank and through the colonial surpluses. As Zwanenberg has observed:

> Very little of the finance was used directly for development of capital; it was instead utilized directly and indirectly, to support inefficient and insolvent white farmers to pay off speculative Lords and Bankers . . . . The racial mystique in Kenya was only the narrowed version of the imperial mystique which had its economic base in the finance capital of the Mother Country. The commercial and merchant banks in Britain were the unregulated instruments of Imperial finance in the colonies, and what appeared to be a fragmentary credit structure of private interests in Kenya in the 1920s was the working out of Imperial finance.[35]

This is well said. These banks included not only Barclays Bank, the Standard Bank of South Africa and the National Bank of India, but also merchandising houses acting as merchant banks, like Arbuthnot and Latham, Mathiesons and Joseph Travers, and many others who advanced loans in order to handle the crop for export. Private moneylenders and rich farmers like the Delameres and Grogans, were also involved. Yet, despite these support measures, the area under maize decreased by 50% between 1929 and 1938. The only sectors that increased were cattle ranching and dairy farming which, with the help of tariff protection and a marketing monopoly, did relatively well, increasing by 80% in this period. A new crop, pyrethrum, was also encouraged from 1935 onwards in the Highlands.

Marketing Modifications

All these measures to assist white capitalist farmers were further supported by the near monopoly held by the farmers in the marketing organization, a fact which came to play a significant part in integrating the total East African economy as a market. The political form of this monopoly was the settler political influence in the committees of the Kenya Legislative Council, which set up bodies for the local control of marketing and for regulating various production activities in the colony.[36] But it is an exaggeration to concentrate on this form of power in isolation from the whole imperialist machinery of control, as Colin Leys' analysis would seem to suggest.[37]

As is already clear from the literature, all these bodies were established to bring certain economies of scale to settler capitalist agriculture, but this was done with the full approval of imperialism as being in its interest; indeed, many of these bodies continued to play more or less the same role much later on under neo-colonialism. The policy of marketing associations and pools, itself a feature of capitalism under imperialism, was used in different forms, even against European companies and in favour of Asian companies (as has been noted by Mamdani).[38]

Despite the fact that settler maize production increased between 1921 and 1930 by 1,800% and the acreage by 800%, output per acre was static at about five to eight bags per acre, depending on the season. The Bowring Committee of 1922 had recommended various measures by which white capitalist agriculture could recover from the ravages of 1919–22, when low prices and the revaluation of the rupee into East African shillings had led to a very considerable loss for the settlers. 'It is therefore not surprising,' as Zwanenberg and King correctly conclude, 'that the Kenya Farmers Association arose out of the needs of European maize producers.'[39]

The British East African Farmers Association, which registered in 1919 and in 1923 changed its name to the Kenya Farmers Association (K.F.A.), was formed with the aim of buying and dealing in cereal crops. It bought from members, graded the product and sold these in bulk for export. Another co-operative marketing association of small farmers in Uasin Gishu plateau competed with the K.F.A., while the Kenya Co-operative Creameries, formed in 1925, catered for milk and butter. When Asian marketing of these and similar agricultural products was removed and farmer associations were given the right to operate in African reserves by the government marketing reforms of 1934, the marketing associations were enabled to buy cheap from the peasants and sell dear outside Kenya, or indeed in the East African market, for local consumption (mainly by African workers and employees). For instance, the K.F.A. bought white settler maize at Shs. 9 per bag, while the same crop bought from African peasants cost them only Shs. 4.90 per bag. The difference was pocketed by the K.F.A. to subsidize settler agriculture. Since the K.F.A. sold maize meal not only in Kenya but in the whole East

African market, it thereby obtained support from these areas for Kenyan white settler agriculture.

The common market across the three territories was, therefore, a vital institution for subsidizing Kenyan high-cost agriculture, particularly when other products like milk, butter, ghee, wheat flour, beef, bread, etc. were taken into account. This was justified in terms of a general distrust for the small trader and the desire to reduce the profits of the middlemen and raise the prices to the 'producers',[40] the peasants and the capitalist farmers. As far as the African peasant producer was concerned, these savings and more went to the state to avoid 'inflation', and in some small degree to the capitalist farmers. In the war period, and particularly after 1938, as we have seen in the case of the other two territories, a new monopoly for marketing under the bulk-purchasing schemes was introduced in Kenya for sugar, sisal, coffee, maize and tea. The K.F.A., the Kenya Coffee Marketing Board and other local marketing monopolies became agents for the Kenya Government and the British Ministry of Food in purchasing these products; prices were fixed by five-year contracts based on production costs.[41]

At the end of the War, a number of new parastatals appeared, dealing, like the K.F.A., in staple foods. The Minister for Agriculture fixed prices, while the existence of the customs union meant that there were also markets in the two other countries, a fact that was to cause conflict within the bilateral system of integration.[42]

Effects of the Second World War
The War had an adverse impact on Kenyan settler production of Arabica coffee. Whereas in 1938 Kenya's coffee accounted for 20% of domestic exports (in value), as against 10% for Uganda and 7% for Tanganyika, the Kenyan margin was very much reduced when her crop acreage contracted from 120,000 to 60,000 during the war years. As a result, Uganda became the major exporter of coffee, demonstrating the resilience of African grown Robusta, and even Bugisu Arabica.[43]

The efforts by British imperialism to maintain supplies for its war effort meant increases in the mechanization of settler agriculture. Using the Lend-Lease facilities extended by the U.S. — which provided an early foothold for U.S. infiltration in the region — the colonial state increased its imports of farm machinery tenfold and mechanization of European farms began in a 'serious fashion' in 1941.[44]

To forward this programme, the colonial state increased farmers' credit facilities for machinery, fertilizers and insecticides. The end of the War saw a renewed effort to encourage white settlers into Kenya, when an Agricultural Settlement Board was set up in 1946 with a loan of £1.5 million raised in London. Uncultivated land owned by former settlers was bought up and new crown land was acquired for this purpose; by 1960 the settler population had more than doubled.

This new settlement implied new capital, as did the strategy of mechanization, with the result that between 1940 and 1960, over £46 million was invested in the Highlands, making possible a considerable increase in output. However, this was still due mainly to an increase in acreage rather than productivity, and explains to some extent the emerging new strategy adopted in relation to African agriculture.

This new policy reflected the general weakening of British imperialism due to the new-found strength of the working class in Britain itself. Further, post-war demand by the British workers and middle classes for increased food and other necessities required a rapid increase in colonial production, which itself provoked an intensification of the anti-colonial struggle in all the oppressed countries − in Kenya, for example, the Mau Mau movement had protested against the robbery of African lands by British imperialism. Finally, Britain's U.S. loan repayments and its dollar shortage in general compelled it to produce more in order to earn hard currencies. All this forced a few liberal moves from the British imperialists in order to weather the winds of change. The appointment of the East African Royal Commission in 1953 to enquire into conditions of land tenure and use in order to bring about better means of farming, the problem being conceived as having resulted from 'increased population', reflects this predicament of British imperialism in the whole area.

The implementation of the new policy took the concrete form of the Swynnerton Plan, which, instead of restricting African agriculture as hitherto or emphasising subsistence farming, urged that African cash crop farming be encouraged on the basis of improved techniques. The existing plots of land, scattered under customary inheritance systems, were to be 'consolidated' into larger units, enabling formal surveying and the granting of title-deeds in order to facilitate credit from banks for such farming. It was argued that this would enable the 'yeoman farmer' to emerge, leading to a change in the social composition of the rural areas towards 'progressive' thinking and habits. The policy was effective to the extent that farming on African-owned lands began to pick up and come to the rescue of British finance capital.

It was also in the interests of the British financial oligarchy to permit some manufacturing in Kenya and, indeed, this formed part of the integration strategy for the entire area. As the World Bank Mission to Kenya observed in 1962: 'The basic policy of the three East African territories, in relation to manufacturing, is to make *East Africa as a whole* self-sufficient in so far as it is possible and economic to do so.'[45] This implied economies of scale calculated with respect to East Africa as a unit and, therefore, the further consolidation of the common market with a common tariff on industrial products.

The needs of British imperialism, spelt out in a number of circulars to the colonial governors on the question of colonial development and welfare in the post-war period, were all connected with the overwhelming need to conserve dollar reserves. This can also be seen in the encouragement of industrialization up to the limit consistent with the competitive position of British monopoly capitalism in a period in which multilateral realignments were already threatening to destabilize the previous pattern of bilateral colonialism. But, under the new international multilateral system, competition between the big nations, and hence their colonies, was soon to set in. Other local factors no doubt contributed to this as mentioned by Zwanenberg and King,[46] and Colin Leys[47] but these in our view fail to take account of the general problem of British imperialism in this period.

Significant as this new policy line might be, most of the new manufacturing was still in the processing of primary products with some limited import substitution, just as earlier manufacturing enterprises had been concerned with the processing of agricultural products, mainly to assist in the overseas marketing of the settler-produced temperate climate foodstuffs. A customs tariff protected these plus any import substitution considered desirable, in relation to the competitive situation of British capital in the world market, and, from 1952, local market possibilities were encouraged under industrial licensing.

The shortages resulting from the Second World War had created the main impetus for intensifying import substitution for the local market in East Africa. This contributed even more to the uneven development of the region, since the logic of British-originated finance capital was to consolidate the dominant position of Nairobi and Mombasa as the industrial bases of the region as a whole.

This dominance by Nairobi was further encouraged by the market, whereby locally processed foodstuffs and beverages were sold to the entire market through the Kenyan-based Marketing Boards and dominated by monopoly interests and local capitalist interests also based in Kenya. Further assistance came from British state capital in the form of the Colonial Development Corporation (C.D.C.), established in 1948 to 'assist the economic development' of the colonial territories.

Earlier, in 1940, a Kenya Industrial Management Board had been set up to encourage the local manufacture of goods that could not be imported during the War. The Board's equipment and plant were subsequently acquired by East African Industries Ltd., a subsidiary of the British monopoly, Unilever, with the assistance of the C.D.C. This company began to manufacture household consumer products like soaps, detergents and cooking oils for the entire East African market. Other industries began to emerge, producing cement, beer, biscuits, metal cans, shoes and pharmaceuticals, most of them based on imported technology, machinery, raw materials and even management personnel, mainly from Britain.

But after the War Britain herself was already being subordinated to U.S.-led multilateral imperialism which was to become much more pronounced in the post-independence period. New forces were showing up in the region in competition with British finance capital. German, Swiss and U.S. finance was quick to cash in on the new order and in a letter from the U.S. International Co-operation Agency to the Permanent Secretary for Commerce and Industry in 1961, it was stated:

As a result of recent discussions with you and other officials in the

Ministry, with Members of the German Mission, and other people, we have decided that such assistance as we will be able to provide, and which the Government of Kenya wishes to employ, could best be directed towards establishing a development bank and the establishment of a research and advisory service intended to stimulate sound, profitable expansion of private enterprise in Kenya.[48]

These new forces of competition implied a new form of integration which we shall examine in Part Two of this volume.

Be that as it may, bilateral integration in the industrial field at this time was further assisted by local institutional arrangements, particularly the industrial licensing bodies set up by British imperialism to co-ordinate investment policy and contain it within the competitive demands of British finance capital. All these productive activities were, of course, part and parcel of the entire financial, commercial and state set-up, closely knit together by the ties of finance capital that formed the logic of the otherwise diverse and apparently contradictory interests. Despite the conflicts in the various institutions and structures, the whole system operated in unison, only counteracted by the forces of revolt at the production and national levels.

References

1. M.P.K. Sorrenson, 'Land Policy in Kenya, 1895–1942' in Harlow, Chilvers and Smith, *History of East Africa* (London, Oxford University Press, 1965).
2. Sorrenson, *op. cit.,* p. 672. Most of what follows concerning land policy and the legal juggling comes from Sorrensen.
3. R. Luxembourg, *The Accumulation of Capital* (London, Routledge and Kegan Paul, 1963), pp. 372–85; see also Palme Dutt, *India Today* (London, Golancz).
4. All this is from Sorrensen, *op. cit.,* pp. 672–6.
5. Lord Lugard, *The Rise of Our East African Empire.*
6. E. Huxley, *White Man's Country: Lord Delamere and the Making of Kenya*, Vol. 1, 1870–1914, (London, Chatto and Windus, 1935) p. 77.
7. *Ibid.,* pp. 77–9.
8. *Ibid.,* pp. 77–9.
9. McDermott, *The British East Africa Company or IBEA* (London, Chapman and Hall, 1895, 2nd ed.), p. 477.
10. R.D. Wolff, *Britain and Kenya 1870–1930: The Economics of Colonialism* (Transafrica, 1974), p. 51.
11. *Ibid.,* p. 52.
12. *Ibid.*
13. *Ibid.*
14. C.C. Wrigley, 'Kenya: The Patterns of Economic Life' in Harlow, Chilvers and Smith, *op. cit.,* Vol. II, p. 214.
15. M.F. Hill, 'The Permanent Way: *The Story of the Kenya and Uganda*

Railway (Nairobi, E.A.R. and H., 1961), pp. 275–6.

16. Sorrensen, *op. cit.,* p. 678.
17. Wolff, *op. cit.,* pp. 63, 65, 85.
18. *Ibid.,* p. 53.
19. Wrigley, *op. cit.,* p. 221.
20. *Ibid.,* p. 224.
21. E.A. Brett, *Colonialism and Underdevelopment in East Africa* (London, Heinemann, 1973), p. 176.
22. *Ibid.,* p. 177.
23. Wrigley, *op. cit.,* p. 233.
24. Brett, *op. cit.,* p. 194.
25. Wrigley, *op. cit.,* pp. 236–7.
26. *Ibid.,* p. 240.
27. *Ibid.,* p. 245.
28. Cmnd. 2387, *Report of the East African Commission, 1925,* pp. 34, 36, 153.
29. R. van Zwanenberg, *Colonial Capitalism and Labour in Kenya, 1919–1939* (Nairobi, East Africa Publishing House, 1975), p. 17, from whom most of this material on the Land Bank is taken.
30. *Ibid.,* p. 19.
31. *Ibid.,* p. 20.
32. *Ibid.,* p. 21.
33. *Ibid.,* p. 23. Zwanenberg brings out well the evidence on this issue, but in our view fails to synthesize it, although he comes to revealing conclusions.
34. Quoted in *ibid.,* p. 25.
35. *Ibid.,* p. 27.
36. C. Leys, *Underdevelopment in Kenya: The Political Economy of Neo-Colonialism* (London, Heinemann, 1975), p. 36.
37. Brett, *op. cit.,* pp. 165–212.
38. M. Mamdami, *Politics and Class Formation in Uganda* (London, Heinemann, 1975), pp. 86–109.
39. R. van Zwanenberg and A. King, *An Economic History of Kenya and Uganda, 1800–1970* (Nairobi, East Africa Publishing House, 1975), p. 204.
40. *Ibid.,* p. 205.
41. Wrigley, *op. cit.,* p. 25.
42. C. Leubuscher, *Bulk Buying from the Colonies* (London, Oxford University Press, 1956).
43. I.B.R.D., *The Economic Development of Kenya: Report of a Mission of the World Bank* (Baltimore, Johns Hopkins, 1963), refers to this situation as 'overboarding' of Kenya, p. 110.
44. Leubuscher, *op. cit.,* pp. 29–30.
45. Zwanenberg and King, *op. cit.,* p. 44; see also generally pp. 44–51 from which most of what follows is taken.
46. I.B.R.D., *op. cit.,* p. 159 (emphasis added).
47. Zwanenberg and King, *op. cit.,* pp. 125–7.
48. Leys, *op. cit.,* pp. 40–127.

5. The End of Colonialism: Political Struggles

In Chapter Four of Volume Two, we analyse in more detail the problems that finally led to the crisis of bilateral imperialism in East Africa under the hegemony of British imperialism. The wearing down of European imperialist powers through imperialist wars and rivalries led increasingly to the weakening of their internal economies, which in turn implied an increasing demand on their colonies' resources. We have seen that in the specific case of East Africa every effort was made by the British imperialists to bring under common control all the resources in the region to sustain Britain during the Second World War.

Thus, the War can be seen as both dealing a crippling blow to the old system of imperial rivalries, and providing the occasion for its greatest efforts at consolidation. The inter-territorial institutions created during the war period became the basis for the further integration of the countries in the region under the East African High Commission. On the imperial scale, the conservation of resources by the colonies and the dominions meant the setting up of the Dollar-Sterling Pool, using the dollar earning of the colonies and dominions for the war effort. We shall see how this pooling meant that the colonies were not paid their foreign exchange earnings. Even when these were converted into usable British sterling, the unavailability of British goods during the War undermined the possible benefits. The peasant producers had large amounts of money deducted from their wages which were retained permanently in the so-called price assistance funds.

Furthermore, these dubious financial manipulations themselves took place in relation to forms of production based on the force of imperialist law and the coercion of almost all the masses of the subjugated peoples. Such exploitation, and the oppression that followed upon it, naturally led to an increasing realization by the people that they had a common enemy. This realization took place at the very roots of economic production and, as exploitation increased, it affected the consciousness of each of the classes emerging within the political economy of East Africa.

The Development of Political Consciousness

Perhaps the earliest consciousness of unity lay in the peasant masses, dispossessed of their livelihood in various degrees and forms — the Kenyan peasantry being the most affected and the Uganda peasantry the least. But it was not the degree of physical dispossession which was at stake so much as being drawn into the colonial market economy. Peasants were required to set aside an increasing amount of labour time for the production of commodities for the market. Instead of producing for their own needs, they were now paid a wage, either working full-time on a settler estate or plantation or on their 'own' plots — 'theirs' in name only. One result of this development was the differentiation between a peasant and a semi-worker or worker; in the latter case this meant an increasing antagonism between worker and exploiter, which manifested itself in the emergence of new forms of struggle, at first patriotic struggles and then sporadic revolts, finally resistances to foreign rule altogether. As the initial revolts failed, imperialism consolidated itself and effected an ever more rigorous economic exploitation of the people, which in turn sharpened this new consciousness.

As the colonial economy became established, new classes and strata emerged among the colonized. With the spread of church school education as part of the recruitment of colonial civil servants, an intellectual petty bourgeoisie began to appear. The previously undifferentiated peasant masses began to be divided into rich and poor peasants, with rich peasants also taking on the newly available role of small traders. Nonetheless these various classes and strata among the exploited and oppressed, with their different types of labour and political organizations were, by 1935, able to converge on certain common aims. By the mid 1940s they were beginning to merge into a kind of national movement, articulating a politics which cut across the classes and strata and striving for a collective consciousness (in the modern age this is called national consciousness), however 'impure', distorted or weak. This alliance represented a real contradiction between two opposing forces, the people and imperialism, and so was able to develop and become better articulated, resulting in the demands of the mid-1950s for 'self-government', and later for national independence and self-determination.

Tanganyika

The first patriotic revolts against German imperialists in Tanganyika took place in the period 1888 to 1895, beginning with 'the Arab Revolt' of 1888 and ending with the revolt of Machemba, a Yao Chief, south west of Lindi. He refused to pay taxes to the Germans and was pursued for five years until 1899 when they finally sent a punitive expedition to put down the revolt and only succeeded in making Machemba flee to the Portuguese territory of Mozambique. In all, no less than 11 revolts took place in these years and were suppressed only with the greatest barbarity on the part of the German imperialists.[1] Nevertheless, that these revolts failed must be attributed to the movement of history which placed German imperialism in a stronger economic position than the weak communal and semi-communal and semi-feudal societies.

With the new economic relationships that had begun to take root, new forms of struggle also became possible and consolidated themselves, beginning with the Maji Maji Rebellion of 1905. This revolt was protracted over two long years of guerrilla warfare and collapsed only when famine devastated the rebel area in 1907.[2] In all, no less than 75,000 people died in this struggle against the exploitative economic conditions imposed by German imperialism, in particular Governor Gotzen's introduction of cotton-growing on the southern coast (after it had failed in the north of the country). The peasants were expected to spend 28 days a year working this *volkscultur* or 'people's crop', for which they were paid such small sums of money that many refused to accept it. The farming considerably interfered with the peasants' subsistence cultivation, and, as Iliffe has concluded:

> Cotton became a grievance which united precisely those people who rebelled when the 1905 picking season began. Several rebel leaders were headmen who had suffered from the scheme, and one of the first rebel actions in any area was commonly to burn the cotton fields. The scheme threatened African economies far more seriously than did any demands by European settlers in the north. It seems sufficient explanation for the outbreak of violence.[3]

Although other ideological elements, such as the religious connotations of the Maji ritual, were used in the rebellion, the revolt can be attributed entirely to the new economic conditions that were imposed on the people, and which were responsible for the basic unity in the entire region under revolt. To the extent that resistance at the level of economic grievance was still new, the revolt was bound to fail. Very soon, however, new forces of opposition to colonial exploitation were taking shape among all the classes emerging in the interstices of the colonial economy. After the Depression, the colonial government's efforts to increase incomes by extending the area of cultivation in the 'Plant More Crops' campaign produced a new source of discontent.

As seen in Chapter Two, it was only the most blatant exploitation of the peasant and plantation worker which kept the British colonial economy going. It is not surprising, then, that a new type of movement, very localized at first, emerged to oppose colonial power. Such movements as the Bukoba Buhaya Union were created in precisely this way, mainly to oppose the new soil conservation and utilization measures forced on the colonial state by soil exhaustion resulting from its 'Plant More Crops' campaign.

Still at this local level, workers' movements like the Kianja Labour Union emerged to protect the interests of workers; such organizations around economic grievances became more prevalent over time. For instance, the 1930s were dominated by movements opposed to the Native Authorities' enforcement of the agricultural and cattle stocking rules.[4] It was with these developments that the peasants began to articulate their grievances and in the course of local struggles managed to create their own leadership.

The workers' movement on the plantations and in the small as well as major towns took longer to become organized into a coherent body. Nevertheless, as is illustrated by the case of the dock-workers and by the life-story of Erica Fiah, by the late 1930s and early 1940s working-class militancy had become part of the Tanganyikan scene.

The rise of a small section of educated Tanganyikans in the early 1920s had already provided another facet of the emergent national forces. Developing in a period that Iliffe calls 'the age of improvement', in which 'Africans concentrated on improving their positions, to face their European rulers on more equal terms', these new social forces pressed for education facilities, economic development and political advance in local government.[5] The agents in this struggle were teachers, clerks and pastors and their organizational weapon was the welfare association.

Such were the roots of the Tanganyika Territory African Civil Service Association (T.T.A.C.S.A.) founded by Martin Kayamba in Tanga in March 1922. This association, although concerned with the interests of its members, acted as a catalyst for other forces at various times. In 1929 it took part in the formation of the Tanganyika African Association (T.A.A.) – the predecessor of the Tanganyika African National Union (T.A.N.U.), the foremost and indeed the only national movement to consolidate itself in Tanganyika. As intellectuals, they began to see Tanganyika as a unit and organized it on that basis.

But such national organization had its base in the strong and emergent peasant movement. As cash crop production developed, a section of the peasantry, along with the rich peasants and the intellectuals, demanded better prices for their products. This concern with marketing led to the growth of the retail co-operative movement, which itself provided necessary economic muscle to the nationalist movement. Agricultural production increased tremendously between 1945 and 1952, with cotton production doubling from 7,512 tons to 14,109 tons, while coffee exports increased their earnings from £896,000 in 1945 to £3,471,000 in 1950 and £6,905,000 in 1955. During this same period pressure from the peasants wrested the concession that marketing co-operatives could be established. In 1945 there were only 79 co-operative societies throughout the whole country; by 1952 this number had risen to 474.

It was in this atmosphere that strong peasant co-operatives like the Victorial Federation increasingly merged their economic role with the political role of the intellectuals. This intellectual force became the focal point for the discontent of all the social classes exploited and dominated by colonialism. In the words of Pratt:

> They gave national focus to the variety of rural discontents which were
> separately agitating many districts. Their activities, and the work of
> their precursors in the African Association, helped to create a national

consciousness which was sufficiently widely shared that the men and women who led local protest movements came easily to the conviction that they ought to give a national expression to this opposition as well. The early nationalists, moreover, provided the leadership and the national organization which were needed to transform this developing anti-colonialism into a major nationalist force in Tanganyika.[6]

The discontent thus catalysed into a national movement opposed to British colonialism was the expression of hostility to the exploitation and oppression of the entire people, and it is for this reason that Pratt is wrong to maintain that this nationalism was not the consequence of 'a widespread undermining of older [i.e. colonial] loyalties nor of the growth of powerful new social classes with aspirations which could not be contained within a colonial system', but more the result of 'new ideas' which had 'permeated into Tanganyika' as a result of education.[7] This leads to a certain idealism in Pratt's explanation of T.A.N.U.'s rise in mass popularity, which he sees as a result of the colonial government's 'unintended support' for T.A.N.U., caused by Governor Twining's decision to delay Tanganyika's advance to representative local councils, and the 'burdensome measures' that were implemented by the Native Authorities with regard to land use and conservation, which we have mentioned above. Pratt concludes that these measures failed because they were 'a mistake', and therefore enabled T.A.N.U. to cash in on the grievances of the peasants in order to emerge as a powerful national movement! This is to put the real situation on its head.

The rise of T.A.N.U. and its struggle for the country's independence from colonial control by British imperialism was itself the dialectical result of the colonial oppression and exploitation of the people of Tanganyika. The success of the people in bringing British imperialism to its knees and forcing it to recognize the right of the people of Tanganyika to self-determination and national independence was a manifestation of the real unity of the people who began to organize themselves into a nation-state entity. This at least allowed them to face future struggles against continued domination by the new multilateral imperialism in a relatively freer atmosphere.

Uganda

In Uganda the earliest revolts against foreign occupation were suppressed with equally tremendous severity. The patriotic armed struggle of the people of Bunyoro under their leader, Kabarega, which occupied the British for no less than nine years of guerrilla struggle, was only put down when Kabarega was shot and wounded. Equally, it was only after a long struggle that the Lamogi Rebellion of 1902, when peasants in Acholi, Lango and Teso resisted British attempts to disarm the population and turn them into wage-slaves, was finally smashed.

The punitive expeditions into the north and east of the country to bring them under colonial administration were also resisted by the people, which called forth fresh repressions. For instance, in 1909 the first Governor of the

Protectorate, Bell, despatching an army unit to Mount Elgon wrote:

> I am sending two companies of the King's African Rifles to make them
> realize that they must come into line with the rest of the protectorate
> . . . . Hardly a year passes without the need of punishing some of these
> wild tribes for the slaying of unarmed and peaceful traders, and nothing
> but a show of force will induce them to mend their ways.[8]

These early revolts were crushed, as in Tanganyika, mainly because of the
economic superiority of the invaders, which enabled them to turn the country
to production for their economic needs. These economic developments were
themselves to call up a new form of opposition.

In Buganda where, under the 1900 Agreement, customary landholding
practices were violated when land was distributed by the colonialists to a
handful of chiefs, this new opposition took the form of resistance to the
comprador chiefs. An association of dispossessed peasants was formed to
demand the reinstatement of the rights of the peasants over the lands and
the recognition of the pre-existing clan institutions.

Since the demands could not be met, the British colonialists decided to
undermine the economic strength of the chiefs and turn them into more
pliant administrators, while at the same time giving the peasants the status
of 'free' producers independent of the chiefs.

In the long run, these reformist measures could not satisfy the peasants
whose new organizations were concerned with the economic issues that
increasingly conditioned the lives of the people. As early as 1913 four rich
peasants in Singo Buganda formed a growers' society to market their own
crops as a co-operative. This was joined by another association in 1923,
whose aims went beyond the mere marketing of crops, to demand the right
to make representations to the government on the peasants' grievances over
the whole oligopolistic structure of marketing.

This atmosphere also created ideal conditions for the emergence of other
types of organization. The Young Baganda Association, formed in 1921,
made demands similar to those of the Tanganyikans in 'the age of improvement', and in other parts of Uganda similar 'welfare' associations were formed.
In Bukedi, Busoga and Bugisu, young intellectual Ugandans demanded
further education for themselves and general improvement in the conditions
of life of the people.

But it was more in the economic field that the newly educated petty
bourgeoisie, particularly in Buganda, began to play a real forceful role among
the peasantry and small traders as well as the workers and small property
owners. This became even more apparent in the 1930s following the reper-
cussions of the Depression in the colony. Large co-operatives like the Uganda
Growers Co-operative Union emerged, and their struggles for recognition by
the state became part of anti-colonialist politics until the 1940s. In 1935 a
Uganda Traders' Union was also formed to advance the interests of small
traders in commerce; the Buganda Merchants' Association appeared in the

same year.

On the more overtly political front, the Bana ba Kintu was formed in 1938 with the aim of organizing the peasants and traders politically. They opposed the clique of comprador chiefs, led by Nsibirwa in Mengo, as a hindrance to the people's struggles. The leading figure at this time was I.K. Musazi who, with other nationalists, tried to unify the political struggles of all the classes. The same year saw the historic founding of the first workers/ lorry owners organization under the name of the Uganda Motor Drivers Association; it was widely recognized as championing the interests of the workers and came to be the first registered trade union in Uganda. James Kivu, the leader of the new organization of workers, collaborated very closely with Musazi, thus linking the peasants, workers and intellectuals in the first major political uprising around the general strike in 1945.

The swiftness and thoroughness of the general strike took the colonial state by surprise and led to a new wave of political protests. The subsequent banning of all existing organizations, and the imprisonment of their leaders, itself led to the formation of new organizations on the economic and political front – organizations like the Bataka Party, formed in 1946, and the Uganda Farmers Union and the Transport and General Workers Union formed in the same year. It was these organizations which provided the main thrust of the 1949 uprising, led by the Bataka Party.[9] In a very real way, therefore, 1949 constituted a watershed in the struggle of the people of Uganda against colonialism. When all the existing organizations of workers were once again banned in that year, the national movement surged forward, calling forth renewed efforts by British imperialism to contain discontent, both at the economic level and through political reforms. The rise of a new type of political party was exemplified by the emergence of the Uganda National Congress in 1952. This nationwide threat to their position in turn led British colonial administration to try and divert the threat by creating local councils representative of local rather than national interests and sentiment.

It is for this reason that the new Governor of Uganda, Andrew Cohen, sent out with a brief to 'harness' nationalist sentiment, pointed out that the 1945 and 1949 disturbances in Buganda were caused by frustrated and discontented elements operating in an atmosphere of economic grievance – a 'typical cause of nationalism'.[10] The new policy of British colonialism should be 'by skilful anticipation to try to guide the energies of nationalists into constructive channels and to secure their co-operation in a programme of steady but not headlong political advance'.[11]

Such 'constructive channels' and 'steady advance' were to be towards neo-colonialism (as we shall see in the next few chapters), but it would be wrong to say the advance was contrived by the colonialists. Theirs was a real response to a real situation posed by the new force of nationalism, which worked steadily towards realizing the objectives of self-determination and national independence. The movement towards neo-colonialism was not itself desired by imperialism, indeed it was a concession to the new forces which marked a new stage in the continuing struggle of the people, which in the future would also be against neo-colonial exploitation and oppression. Uganda's realization of its objective on 9 October 1962 marked such a new stage.

Kenya

As we have noted earlier, the struggles of the people of Kenya were focused right from the beginning upon the dispossession of their lands by the colonialists. However, while the agrarian question formed a very important aspect of the national struggle and of national and colonial questions in general, it was the exploitation of the workers and poor peasantry at the level of colonial production which provided the impetus to the movement; the agrarian issue was linked from an early stage with the labour question.

But in Kenya, as elsewhere in East Africa, the first patriotic resistance was violently crushed. The first resistances on the coast by the Arabs and Swahilis began in the late 1880s and ended with the Mazrui War of 1895, followed up by British military campaigns. In the interior the seizure of lands from the people by the colonial state provided the first material basis for the revolts of the Nandi, Kikuyu and Masai people. The troublesome Nandi were dealt with in a series of British punitive expeditions and raids in 1895, 1900, 1902, 1903 and finally as late as 1905. The last campaign required 12 companies of the King's African Rifles, along with 1,000 Masai levies.[12] The Nandi's efforts to resist ended in defeat and the loss of livestock and the greater part of their lands to the British invaders.

Since the land was from the very beginning the most burning issue, even the chiefs recruited by the colonialists to serve the colonial state found themselves bound by the popular pressure of the masses to take up some of their grievances. Inevitably, the land question was the central area of concern of the first African organization in Kenya in 1919, the Kikuyu Association, led by Chief Koinange and other chiefs, including Josiah Njonjo, Philip Karanja, Mathew Njoroge and Waweru wa Mahoi.

These land agitation organizations were joined very early in the history of East Africa by a new kind of organization in which the workers began to play a leading role in putting not only their own case, but that of the peasants and other sections of the population. The first was the Young Kikuyu Association, formed in 1921 by Harry Thuku, a telephonist in the colonial treasury, which had among its main objectives the representation of African grievances to the government in matters of workers' wages, the carrying of passes (*kipande*) by the Africans, and the land issue. Thuku declared:

> When we went to do porter war work [as porters in the Carrier Corps] we were told by His Excellency the Governor that we should be rewarded. But is our reward to have our tax raised and to have registration papers given to us and for our ownership of our land to be called in question; to be told today that we are to receive title deeds and tomorrow for it to appear that we are not to receive them?[13]

Later in the same year, it was realized by Harry Thuku and others that, in order to succeed, Africans not only in Kenya but in East Africa as a whole must organize together. So in July of that year they decided to rename the Young Kikuyu Association the East African Association. This was a significant step and the settlers' newspaper, the *Leader*, of 7 July 1921 was quick to blame such a development on 'Asiatic claims' for equality, and 'the better organized Baganda political section' for efforts 'towards political and industrial organization'.[14] Later, when this Association was banned and its leaders, including Harry Thuku, deported, the Kenyan colonial authorities required the Association to change its name to the Kikuyu Central Association, in order to give it a 'tribal' orientation.

Meanwhile, the anti-colonialist movement was building up in the whole country. In 1921, at a meeting attended by over 8,000 people, the Kavirondo Association was formed, demanding that the colonial government allow representation, end the Hut Tax and the *kipande* system, provide education, remove the designation of Kenya as a 'colony', pay full wages for all work performed by the people for the government in the reserves, and grant title deeds to the people for their lands as security against confiscation by the settlers.

All these demands were connected with the contradictions introduced into the country by the new relations of production, and the inevitable banning of these organizations produced further political developments. The banning of the East African Association in 1924, for instance, produced a gigantic protest by the people in the biggest strike and demonstration yet seen in Kenyan history. The use of the King's African Rifles infuriated the people and a riot broke out leading to the death of at least 150 people.[15]

Even the formation of the Kikuyu Central Association (K.C.A.) in 1925, essentially as a colonialist move to take the steam out of the nationalist movement, did not succeed in damping the spirit of nationalism. In the words of Makhan Singh, the change in the name of the East Africa Association was, as far as the people were concerned, simply a tactic 'so that political activity in the interests of all Africans could be continued and conducted openly'.[16] On this basis the K.C.A. began to mobilize the people on 'the burning problems of land, labour and other questions of national interest', such as education, forced labour, wages and African representation on the Legislative Council, all of which, 'in spirit', were the national policies of the East Africa Association.[17]

For the next 16 years, the K.C.A. was the only political organization which was actively involved in national politics, despite its new 'tribal' name. In 1928 it began a mouthpiece group with the significant name of *Mwiguithania* (the Unifier) and helped to establish sister organizations which were also compelled to operate on an ethnic basis by the colonialists. The formation of such bodies as the Baluya (Kavirondo) Taxpayers Welfare Association, Wakamba (Ukamba) Members Association and Wateita (Teita Hills) Association, were efforts by the K.C.A. to create a national movement out of the scattered units that colonialism imposed.

The K.C.A. engaged in various forms of struggle, all intended to heighten the people's consciousness of foreign domination; for example, it backed the squatters' struggles for more land. By the 1940s it had attracted the wrath of the colonial regime and was proscribed on the grounds that it was in contact with the King's enemies in Ethiopia. With the arrest of its leaders and those of the other associations, the K.C.A. moved to operate underground until 1944 when the leaders were released. In that year, a more broadly-based movement, the Kenya Africa Union (K.A.U.) , was formed

> to unite the people of Kenya; to prepare the way for the introduction of democracy in Kenya; to defend and promote the interests of the African people by organizing, educating and leading them in the struggle for better working conditions, housing, etc.; to fight for equal rights for all Africans; to break down all racial barriers; to strive for the extension to all African adults the right to vote and be elected . . .; to publish a political newspaper periodically; to fight for freedom of assembly, press, movement; and to raise and administer the funds necessary to affect these objects (Constitution).[18]

On this basis the K.A.U. became the new spokesman for the struggle of the people of Kenya, articulating the grievances and taking a lead in the preparations for the Mau Mau Revolution brewing in the Kenya Highlands over the agrarian issue of the squatters. The formation of the Land and Freedom Army signalled the arrival of militant and armed nationalism that characterized Kenya's independence struggle.

The banning of K.A.U. and other organizations did not help the colonial regime. The arrests of its leaders only inflamed the people's national passion, thus intensifying the armed resistance. By the late 1950s, it was already clear that British colonialism could no longer hamper the progress of the struggle of the people against it, just as it had failed in other areas of the world and, by 1963, it was being forced to accept the judgment of history: recognition of the right of the people of Kenya to national independence.

References

1. J.F. Rweyemamu, *Underdevelopment and Industrialization in Tanzania* (Nairobi, Oxford University Press, 1973), pp. 12–13.
2. J. Iliffe, *Tanganyika Under German Rule* (Nairobi, East Africa Publishing House, 1969), p. 20.
3. *Ibid.*, p. 23.
4. L. Cliffe, 'Nationalism and the Reaction to Enforced Agricultural Change in Tanganyika During the Colonial Period' in J. Saul and L. Cliffe (eds.), *Socialism in Tanzania* (Nairobi, East Africa Publishing House, 1972).
5. J. Iliffe, 'Tanzania Under German and British Rule' in *ibid.*, pp. 11–13.

6. C. Pratt, *The Critical Phase in Tanzania 1945-1968* (London, Oxford University Press, 1976), p. 23.
7. *Ibid.*, pp. 24-35.
8. A.D. Low, 'The Protectorate 1894-1919' in Harlow, Chilvers and Smith (eds.), *History of East Africa* (London, Oxford University Press, 1965), pp. 105-6.
9. For an account of these developments, see D.W. Nabudere, *Imperialism and Revolution in Uganda* (London/Dar es Salaam, Onyx Press/Tanzania Publishing House, 1979), Ch. VII.
10. A. Cohen, *British Policy in Changing Africa* (London, Routledge and Kegan Paul, 1970), pp. 34-5.
11. *Ibid.*, p. 61.
12. R.D. Wolff, *Britain and Kenya: 1870-1930*, (Nairobi, Transafrica, 1974), p. 63.
13. Quoted in Makhan Sing, *History of Kenya's Trade Union Movement to 1952* (Nairobi, East Africa Publishing House, 1969), p. 11.
14. *Ibid.*, p. 12.
15. *Ibid.*, p. 16.
16. *Ibid.*, p. 25.
17. *Ibid.*
18. Quoted in Barnett and Njama, *Mau Mau from Within* (New York, Monthly Review, 1966), p. 39.

Part Two
Neo-Colonialism and Transnational Integration

6. The Rise of Multilateralism and Neo-Colonialism

Multilateral imperialism can be defined as modern imperialism operating within the narrowing horizons created by the emergence of the socialist system marked by the October Revolution.[1] This meant a new phase of modern imperialism, but one still representing the highest stage of capitalism based on exports of capital by the monopolies in the imperialist states to each other and to the 'backward' areas.

The earlier phase of modern imperialism, what we have called 'bilateral imperialism', was characterized by sharp national rivalries over colonies, eventually resulting in two world wars. The Second World War saw the disintegration of these old colonial possessions, from which the U.S. gained considerably, enabling it to impose its own division of the world based on the accessibility of open door neo-colonialism to the hegemony of finance capital and production. A system of multilateral institutions was worked out to guarantee this new division of the world, accompanied by a new level of monopolistic competition reflecting the greater degree of concentration and centralization of capital based on the transnational corporate arrangement. But, just as with 'old-style' bilateral imperialism, military arrangements were made to back it up.

To understand the new developments in East African integration, this major structural alteration must be grasped; otherwise, our analyses will remain merely descriptive.

Before the end of the Second World War it was increasingly obvious that U.S. finance capital was emerging as the strongest in the world capitalist system. With the other imperialist states fighting to retain their existing possessions and badly in need of the material resources to do so, it was only natural for the U.S. to increase its production potential and reinforce its already bulging economy. With its G.N.P. double that of the pre-war period, and able to export one-third of the world's manufactured goods while only importing one-tenth, U.S. gold reserves were bound to increase severalfold from $0.4 billion in 1932 to $20 billion by the 1950s. The U.S. share of world capital exports also rose: from 6.3% in 1914 to 35.3% in 1935 and to well over 45% by the end of the War, while Britain's share fell from 50.3% to 43.8% to 24.5% over the same period.[2]

Thus the U.S. emerged as the champion of 'open door' neo-colonialism.

Its policy, worked out while the other imperialists fought, was to advocate multilateralism as against bilateralism, condemning the colonialism of the European powers and supporting the colonies' 'right to self-determination'. This was precisely the policy suited to its own plan to redivide the world.

Transnational Corporate Strategy

A marked feature of multilateral imperialism was the further development in concentration of capital and production on a world scale by the monopolies. The first transnational corporations to appear on the scene were U.S. multinationals, soon joined by European and Japanese monopolies which, without a global corporate structure, had to struggle to compete in the world market.

This strategy — itself a form of concentration of capital — was further necessitated by the fact that political situations in the neo-colonial world did not lend themselves to *direct* political, and hence economic, control by particular imperialist powers. To compete in such environments required on-the-spot representation of the monopoly in one form or another in the neo-colonial state itself. It is in this sense that the transnational corporate structure was the one most suited to the monopolistic competition in the new environment. What was this structure?

A characteristic of the transnational corporation was its centralized organization, reflecting the level of concentration necessary for the increasingly high levels of profitability required to sustain the operation. This crisis of falling profitability, itself a reflection of the concentration of and higher organic composition of capital on a world scale, had itself been the major factor in the inter-imperialist wars leading up to the U.S. redivision of the world. The crisis had taken place despite the operation of the pre-1945 cartel and monopoly trust structure. It was precipitated by the breakdown of colonial relationships, whereby monopolies had worked through colonial enclaves and tariff barriers to divide markets and find ready outlets for capital exports. To maintain a higher-than-average profitability a new structure was necessary for the monopoly firm, a structure which did not rely on protected colonial enclaves and tariff-barricaded home markets — which the multilateral arrangement had itself dismantled. That the U.S. monopolies should lead in this rearrangement was not surprising, given their already high level of concentration and high organic composition of capital.

Since multilateralism allowed the U.S. greater freedom of movement for its capital and goods at a time when the other imperialist powers were weakened, it did not need to fear their competition. U.S. pressure for an end to direct colonialism by the European powers was thus merely a way of asserting its own hegemony in entering those markets. The creation of a neo-colonial order would enable it to exercise greater control over the world's resources and markets without any need to colonize those countries directly. To achieve multilateralism the U.S. even went to the extent of giving loans to the European powers to rebuild their economies, precisely in order to set up the new system which it was sure to dominate.

In Point IV of the Atlantic Charter, signed during the War by the U.S. and Britain, it was declared that all the signatories 'will endeavour . . . to further the enjoyment by all states, great or small, victor or vanquished, of access, on equal terms, to the trade and to the raw materials of the world which are needed for their economic prosperity'. The rationale behind this policy, according to Richard Gardner, was the concern that the world wars had been caused by 'unequal opportunity' of access to these resources. 'Closed trade areas controlled by imperial powers were held to deny other countries their natural rights [*sic*] to the vital raw materials, markets and investment outlets.'[3]

So it can be seen that what the U.S. demanded ultimately was power to exercise its 'natural right' to share in the exploitation of the labour and resources of the backward areas which Europe had previously dominated. With the achievement of political independence by countries formerly under direct colonial rule, the U.S. was well placed to take full advantage of the weakness of their national democratic forces and their fragile independence to assert its own economic hegemony in competition with the erstwhile imperialist powers.

A powerful weapon in this bid for control was the aid hand-outs to the new neo-colonial states: U.S. monopolies were thus able to move in as 'friends', bringing with them investment for 'development' on a 'non-communist' path. We have seen how this aid in fact started even before the end of colonialism in East Africa, particularly directed towards agriculture, providing credit to African farmers and assisting small traders. But most of this new 'aid' consisted, in effect, of a form of strategic assistance intended to bolster the new colonial regimes against 'communism'. In this way the U.S. imperialists hoped to establish themselves with a section of the local bourgeoisie as their comprador force to resist any further struggles for the consolidation of national independence. Despite the all too evident success of this policy, it was soon challenged by the forces of national liberation which today continue to press for an end to imperialist exploitation and domination. With the failure of the U.S. imperialists to maintain their hegemony in Vietnam and Indo-China as a whole, it has become clearer that the contradictions of multilateral imperialism are coming more and more to the fore.

Indeed, on a deeper level of historical analysis, it is obvious that this development itself reflects the level of evolution of the capitalist firm. Initially, the capitalist firm catered for the home market and then exported the excess product, the excess being determined by the stage of technological development and capital mobilization (centralization). Overseas operations were centralized in the home country and viewed as subordinate and supplementary to the home activities. The later development of the international firm was to reverse this order of priorities and emphasize overseas investment and markets by making them more autonomous and enabling the cartel system to operate internationally. This form of the international firm in turn gave way to the transnational corporation that emerged with multilateral imperialism. The transnational monopoly no longer drew a distinction between home and foreign activities, but saw domestic activity as itself subordinate to and fully integrated with the global structure and strategy of the transnational enterprise. This strategy consisted essentially in the elimination of competition as far as possible on the international scale, thus producing a monopolistic structure geared to removing barriers to the centralization of all the factors of production on a world scale through the operations of the objective economic laws of monopoly in order to reap super-profits. The export of capital in all its forms — money, machinery and know-how — was now tied to the control of sources of raw materials and markets.

Since most technology for the manufacture of mass consumption goods was by this time highly standardized, and thus open to replication by other countries, advantage over other monopolies would be obtained either by historical claims on particular markets and raw material bases or by presenting the most attractive 'package' of factors of production. In such packages the dominant monopoly would ensure lower-cost production consistent with the conditions in its home country and overseas. Finance coupled with control over technology (i.e. machinery, equipment and know-how) now offered the best chance for mobilizing other resources wherever it operated, allowing for very high profits in relatively backward areas with a lower organic composition of capital.

Thus a transnational finance capital, with its corporate plan for all its activities on a world scale, views operations in one overseas market as only a small segment of its global activities. It invests at a 'loss' in some areas in order to defend its market or source of raw materials; by thus protecting its outlets for capital exports it is able to mobilize local resources. This means that it has to make above average profits (super-profits) elsewhere, in order to sustain these 'losses'. Above all, its overseas profits must be substantially greater than those at home.

The determination of the rate of profit to be expected in particular localities depends on calculations as to the risks involved. This entails investigating the size of the market, investment climate, costs, labour conditions, incomes, population, production, imports and exports, labour power and other relevant factors. Where a substantial risk is involved, the monopoly will insist on a pay-back period of three to five years.[4] In such situations it may also demand special incentives from the client neo-colonial state — for example, tax reliefs, low-interest loans, easy repatriation of earnings, high tariffs for import-substitution production, lax import and exchange controls, and controlled labour unions.

A variety of means will be used to achieve these objectives: joint ventures with local capital, either state capital or private capital, or management, technical, financial and marketing agreements. These arrangements enable it first to mobilize local resources for, as Dymsza has correctly pointed out, 'It combines transmitted scarce resources in producing, distributing, and marketing goods and services'.[5] Second, these strategies imply prior claims to local management skills and skilled labour in particular. Third, they guarantee easier access to raw materials, markets and systems of distribution, including state systems. Fourth, local loans, tax incentives and importation of raw materials will be facilitated. All these and other benefits obtained through joint ventureship enable the transnational corporation to minimize risks while, at the same time, maintaining effective control over the whole enterprise, even as a minority interest.

In this way neo-colonial economies quickly find themselves bound up in a web-like control by huge capitalist monopolies continuing in a new form the imperialist economic control over their resources. We will see that the new forms of integration that characterized the East African political economy in this period were consistent with this outline of the operations of transnational corporations as rooted in the new economic discipline of the multilateral institutional system.

The Multilateral Institutional System

The three multilateral institutions created after the War – the World Bank, the International Monetary Fund and the General Agreement on Trade and Tariffs – were involved in the planning of the East African economies even before the collapse of colonialism. The details of the handover to the new system, to be supervised by these institutions, will be traced in the next section. Here we shall briefly sketch the functions of each of these institutions and their interaction in supervising and managing the world economy of imperialism in which the neo-colonial world now took its place. Although these institutions were formally separate, they collaborated in carrying out their functions.

The I.B.R.D. or the World Bank was the multilateral institution called in to assess East African resources available for 'future development' in the first real effort to bring the three territories under a new form of economic management. Described as a 'bridge over which private capital could move into the international field',[6] it served international finance capital by setting in motion the mobilization and deployment of multilateral capital for the development of infrastructure, transport and mining.

Through sister organizations like the International Finance Corporation (I.F.C.) and the International Development Association (I.D.A.), the World Bank pumped finance capital into private companies and governments. It demanded in return the most favourable incentives and situations for the profitable investment of finance capital and its repatriation with profits.

The activities of the World Bank were closely co-ordinated with those of another multilateral institution, the International Monetary Fund (I.M.F.). The financial and monetary advice offered by the I.M.F. had to be implemented before loans were made by the World Bank. The I.M.F.'s main function was to stabilize international currencies, including those of the

Third World, ensuring their free convertibility. In assisting a country with its balance of payments, the I.M.F. could, and often did, argue a policy line that helped finance capital flow more freely and operate more profitably: when governments were encouraged to devalue their currencies, monopolies could purchase the products of the Third World countries cheaply; when they were urged to eliminate controls on foreign exchange and increase tax benefits, the monopolies once again benefited.

The World Bank sent teams of 'expert' planners from time to time to Third World countries to set up development projects and appraisal surveys as well as to make recommendations for investment patterns along the lines suggested above. In its monetary and currency policies the I.M.F. tried to ensure a freer flow of international trade by ensuring a fully convertible currency, and in this latter task it was assisted by the General Agreement on Trade and Tariffs (G.A.T.T.).

G.A.T.T.'s terms of reference were to ensure the most favourable conditions of international trade for all its members on a non-discriminatory basis. It aimed at eliminating trade barriers, lowering tariffs and removing, or at least containing, quantitative controls which would decrease international trade or create discrimination. Here the I.M.F. played its part in supervising exchange controls and restrictions which also tended to affect trade. Originally conceived as a body that could assist development of Third World countries 'through trade', G.A.T.T. soon found this clearly out of the question, and its role developed into one of ensuring that these countries continued to play the role of raw material suppliers with a minimum of processing and semi-processing. It also regulated the formation of customs unions and 'free-trade' areas, under which regional arrangements of the East African type could be further supervised to ensure no discriminatory arrangements which might operate against the multilateral arrangements.

The effects of these functions of the multilateral institutions will be shown to be relevant to our analysis of the new forms of integration which replaced the institutions of bilateral imperialism. In the post-colonial period, these new forms of multilateral integration advanced, assisted by the I.B.R.D., the I.M.F. and G.A.T.T. Capital continued to concentrate on a world scale and the structures capable of sustaining a new and intensified monopolistic competition for the world's resources were given a new lease of life.

The transnational corporations which thrived on this competition, and in whose interests the new forms of integration were being created, took full advantage of these institutional arrangements to integrate the productive activities of the three East African countries into their global monopoly activities. The neo-colonial states thus continued to be exploited economically and their own policies functioned as instruments for the continued oppression of the people of East Africa.

Multilateral Institutions and Neo-Colonialism in East Africa

The three World Bank missions[7] which surveyed the region's economies were essentially agreed on the retention of the East African institutional arrangement as a basis for its future economic development. This was in line with the wishes of the existing British monopolies and of the British Government, which at that time still exercised political control. In any case, there was no conflict between these institutional arrangements and the new system of multilateralism in which Britain was itself involved.

But the missions also expressed certain reservations about its future. While acknowledging the usefulness of the common market, the Tanganyika Report indicated certain disadvantages and losses of revenue and industrial development resulting from it.[8] The Uganda Report was more emphatic that any economic benefit would depend upon a political integration involving a common fiscal policy for East Africa as a whole.[9] The Kenya Report also expressed reservations by refraining from making any recommendations which 'if adopted, would impede the governments of the East African countries from making such changes in their political relationships as they might consider desirable'.[10] In its substantive recommendations the World Bank made every effort to ensure the future development of these countries as outposts for the export of capital by the monopolies, by encouraging both private and state participation in certain areas.

Tanganyika

The Tanganyika Report pointed out that, while Tanganyika's development had been aided by capital inflow, Tanganyika itself had made substantial contributions to the financing of its own development through taxes from export earnings. (Its capital formation has been rather high for its *per capita* income.) While it could be argued that two-thirds of domestic capital formation came from the private sector and one-third from the public sector, these proportions would be reversed when the subsistence investment component of the private sector was recognized. With this adjustment it became apparent that the public sector accounted for over 40% of capital formation, while private capital accounted for less than 60%, concentrated mostly in the service sector with some investment in manufacturing, construction and agriculture. The importance of the government's role in economic development became clear once it was understood that much of its recurrent expenditure also went into productive activities. The Report concluded:

> It will be apparent from what has been said above that the pace and shape of future development in Tanganyika are highly dependent on public action, notably in the central task of improvement and transformation of African agriculture, in providing, improving and maintaining communications over the large distances of the territory and in 'investment in people', notably education . . . . Even taking into account grants which Tanganyika receives at present, chiefly from the

United Kingdom, and the sums which the Government of Tanganyika can borrow, limitation of financial resources remains the main restriction on the public development effort and hence, to a major degree, on development of the economy as a whole.[11]

The central problem of Tanganyika was, therefore, 'how much to borrow' on soft terms. Noting that the London money market was very competitive and pointing to the possibility of the World Bank advancing the money (although it warned that the terms would be 'similar'), the Report framed its recommendations for agricultural development and industrial development accordingly.

In the case of agriculture, it pointed out that Tanganyika differed from Kenya, where overcrowding and fragmentation of land had reached a stage involving hardships for the majority of farmers. In Tanganyika the problem was to increase production on planned holdings, increasing yields per acre rather than increasing acreage by methods which deplete fertility of the soil. Although the ultimate goals of the 'improvement' and 'transformation' programmes were the same, the mission recommended the 'transformation' approach, consisting of the planned settlement of empty areas, rather than exclusive concentration on improvement of methods in already settled areas. This shift to new areas was seen as a way of making people more receptive to changes. 'Where people are under pressure to move or see the advantage of doing so, they can be required to abide by rules and to adopt new practices as a condition of receiving new land.'[12] So it can be seen that Tanzania's subsequent rural policy was being laid down well ahead of time.

The line on industrialization was no less clear. The Report noted that the 300 establishments employing 50 or more people were private companies and large firms which had recently moved into Tanganyika as branches of enterprises already established in Kenya. Although the large firms were few, they accounted for three-quarters of the value of manufacturing, and most of the recent investment — about £1.75 million a year. Nonetheless, it was argued that the government should form some idea of the path which future development in industry should take, albeit that the market determined 'the outside limits' to such expansion.

Because of the *de facto* customs union in East Africa and the already existing developments in Kenya's industrialization, it was difficult to think of many manufactures that might be developed in Tanganyika in the near future for sale in the East African market as a whole.[13] Nevertheless, the Report indicated that there were opportunities for 'displacing existing imports' of manufactures for certain commodities which had a 'mass market' in the country, and 'which appear capable of being produced at costs which, if not fully competitive with imports in all cases, are at least in the range requiring a relatively low degree of protection'.[14]

The Report recommended a 'moderate' level of tariff protection for this purpose, and pinpointed beer, cigarettes, cement, sugar, textiles, footwear, rubber tyres and tubes as the 'most promising' mass commodities for import substitution. It recommended the abolition of the system of industrial licensing, which appeared to serve no useful purpose. The post-war developments of industries like cement, cigarettes and footwear supported the view that, once the scope of the market was sufficient, business enterprises were prepared to risk their capital in non-scheduled industries without official assurance of protection against competition. This argument was important in preparing the way for new forms of monopolistic competition.

The Report noted that the Tanganyikan Government did not itself operate any enterprises, while its participation in joint ventures with private enterprise had been limited on an *ad hoc* basis. It recommended the establishment of an investment corporation to attract foreign capital and noted that the Colonial Development Corporation had promised expertise for setting up an 'investigatory company' to appraise opportunities for development, while a sum of money for an industrial development corporation had been voted in the budget. This would assist in promoting small-scale enterprise and funding research, as well as acting as a financial partner with local capital.[15]

Uganda

The Report of the World Bank mission to Uganda also laid the foundations for a neo-colonial economy. The mission's main task was specifically to 'present practical recommendations' which were to serve as 'the basis for a development programme covering the period 1961/62–1965/66'. Its Report laid down the 'Approach Strategy and Programme' for carrying out the specific actions recommended. In the 'Approach' it was pointed out that, short of another 'windfall in export earnings', Uganda would need to borrow money on competitive terms, and to achieve this there would have to be 'fair treatment' of existing investment and the creation of a 'feeling of stability and security in the next few years'. This would not only stop the flight of capital but eventually attract more.

The 'Strategy' pointed to the need to attain a 5% rate of growth by increasing 'direct wealth-creating activities' and the eventual transition from the 'subsistence way of life' to a modern monetary economy. The 'programme' proposed a budget for agriculture and industry, emphasising the former. The local capital content of the budget was estimated at 48%, while the balance was to come from external sources.[16]

In the field of agriculture the Report emphasized the need to diversify. The reliance on coffee as the major crop should be supplemented by more cotton production. Forms of agriculture should also be changed, with the partnership of large estates and peasant production in the form of 'outgrower schemes', and support for the 'progressive farmer' (i.e. rich peasant) by credits and subsidies; group farms for cotton growing were also to be encouraged.

The Report noted that, in an economy 'such as Uganda', the chief industries were based directly on agricultural production because modest purchasing power limited the demand for the products of secondary industries. It noted the existence of a number of industries, protected by the long distance from the coast, and remarked that the government held the majority of shares in the Uganda Development Corporation (U.D.C.), which was not only 'the biggest single industrial organization in the country',[17] but the only producer of cement, textiles and enamelled metalware. Through other subsidiaries it controlled a number of tea estates, a cattle ranch, a chain of modern hotels and National Park Lodges and several leasehold properties. In association with overseas firms, the U.D.C. participated as a minority shareholder in hire-purchase banking, mining ventures, food processing and the production of specialized building materials. While aware of the role of private companies in manufacturing, the Report nevertheless pointed to the growing importance of the U.D.C. as a holding company. Referring to the existing common market arrangement, it argued that the continuance of the market was in the interests of East Africa and of Uganda.

According to the Report, Uganda's problem in the industrial sphere was 'how to manoeuvre to its own advantage within the limits imposed by a uniform tax structure and a common tariff code'.[18] Tax incentives like customs duty refunds should be used and new industry should be protected; tax 'holidays' should also be considered. In line with the Tanganyika mission, the Report also recommended the abolition of the industrial licensing system.[19]

Kenya

The Kenya mission's task was to undertake a general review of the economic potential of Kenya and to make recommendations designed to assist the government in developing a plan for the period up to 1967 and to formulate policies which would further expand and stimulate the economy. The Report emphasized that Kenya 'must adopt a programme for development in the public sector to give emphasis to activities with the highest potential returns, and measures to stimulate and encourage expansion of production in the private sector'.[20] But such measures would 'come to nought' unless steps were 'first taken to restore confidence', to remove 'as soon as possible' the present uncertainties as to political and social conditions.

The programme for economic development in agriculture advised the continuation of the basic line laid down in the Swynnerton Plan, consisting 'mainly [of] land consolidation, enclosure and the development of cash production in the non-scheduled areas' (i.e. former African reserves). Specific changes in policy were recommended for each crop. It warned that the pressure for settlement in the scheduled areas (i.e. the former White Highlands) and the uncertainty about the future among white farmers would lead to a decline in production and export earnings in the years immediately ahead. This loss could retard the progress of the country as a whole: 'We hope that the introduction of the high density settlement scheme will help to restore confidence, but in any case there is urgent need for measures specifically designed to revive investment in agriculture.'[21]

As regards industrialization, the Report particularly emphasized that any expectations of expansion in manufacturing industry depended 'mostly on private initiative'. Although government assistance was required, 'Generally, we do not think that an extension of the role of Government in production is required and we doubt whether it would be beneficial during the next few years.'[22] It was recommended that an Industrial Development Corporation be established, but solely for the purpose of providing finance and information to private enterprise. It is important to note how the Kenyan policy line differed from those recommended for Uganda and Tanganyika. It was to have considerable implications for the type of integration that was to emerge in East Africa in this period as we shall see in the next few chapters. The Report continued:

> The expansion of manufacturing depends partly on the establishment of a favourable climate for investment. Conditions likely to promote the further development of production in private hands include a clear statement of policy toward private investment, reassurances about [non] interference by the state with private undertakings, freedom of transfer of earnings and repatriation of original capital abroad.[23]

To this extent specific government assistance was 'especially required to encourage the growth of industries which could be well located in East Africa to displace imports'. It recommended customs concessions, tax incentives, protective duties, etc. to encourage such private investment.

The Region as a Whole

Through these 'neutral' multilateral positions of the World Bank, which in fact laid the groundwork for open door neo-colonialism — 'open' particularly to U.S. monopolistic activities — changes were made in the framework of the competition for British bilateral imperialism. More and more U.S. and other monopolies were cashing in on the political changes that had taken place in the region. The sentiments of the U.S. monopolies were reflected in a Report prepared by U.S.A.I.D.[24] to help the Tanganyika Ministry of Planning draw up an overall plan for industrial development. It pointed out that it lagged behind because of discrimination *within* the East African common market. East Africa's financial institutions, common market administrators and skilled technicians were concentrated in Nairobi where they could 'get on the blower' to each other and settle matters through the 'old boy network'. It continued: 'The "old boy net" survives as a barrier to Tanganyika's development even though its original purpose has been lost and many of the "old boys" have gone home.'[25] It gave many examples of projects proposed for Tanganyika's development which had been turned down by the 'old boys' in Nairobi, and proposed 126 industrial opportunities 'at least', which could be established in Tanganyika. It advocated the setting up of small industries run by the Tanganyikan 'negroes' and advised that loans to assist them could come from agencies such as itself where it was possible to obtain a 10- or 20-year revolving credit. It pointed out that, although some of these loans were tied to procurements from the U.S., it was possible for part of the loan to be used for local procurements.

U.S. capital equipment is not well known in East Africa, and some
types would be more expensive than equipment from Europe. However,
with the help of U.S. technical assistance it should be possible to
identify some that would be economically desirable. Examples might
be garage equipment, radio test sets, slaughtering, freezing and canning
equipment, lorries/trucks and omnibuses, etc.

Furthermore the threat of loss of East African markets to U.S.
competitors might stimulate European countries to make their own
tied loans available . . . . For instance, the U.K. might want to provide
financing for lorries and omnibuses, along the lines of the recent loans
to Cuba . . . .[26]

In short, the Report concluded, 'Tanganyika needs to develop its own new
"old boy net"' — in fact, a new U.S. package to compete with the old British
one. It is clear that U.S. imperialism was advocating the dismantling of the
old structures in favour of ones which would be amenable to its own monopolistic competition. This was a new phase in developments in East Africa —
a phase that was to be characterized by new dominant economic forces that
were to shape the future of the regional institutions in the absence of strong
local economic forces. Step by step, the economies of East Africa were taken
over by the new forces of competition which increasingly affected the conditions under which the old British finance capital could operate in the
region.

The Struggle Between Bilateral and Multilateral Imperialism

The neo-colonial economies that emerged on the basis of the multilateral
strategy just outlined conformed to the interests of all the imperialist monopolies, British finance capital no longer being the sole determinant of the
economic situation. The region was integrated *multilaterally* at the level of
production, with all the imperialist monopolies exporting their capital to
exploit East African labour and resources. Institutional arrangements from
the bilateral period were adapted to this new purpose. Institutions which
did not respond easily were discarded and new ones, not necessarily regional,
set up to advance the new exploitation that was being imposed on the region
by the U.S.-led multilateral imperialism.

The weakness of British finance capital was demonstrated by its timidity
in the face of the more powerful monopolistic forces appearing in the arena.
Some of its capital had already fled the territories; and even though the
forces of national liberation had only just begun to show their strength, it
was sufficient to cause further dismay in the minds of some British investors.
However, the working class and poor peasantry, the most exploited classes
and the real antithesis to finance capital and imperialism, were still weak and
unorganized *as classes*. This now enabled multilateral imperialism to enforce
its new forms of exploitation on the people.

The hesitancy of British monopolies to invest new capital without re-assurances of the kind demanded by the World Bank missions can be seen in the results of a survey carried out in 1965 by D.J. Morgan for the British Overseas Development Institute Ltd.[27] He reported that British business was, on the whole, leaving Africa to U.S. finance capital and exporting its capital elsewhere, despite the fact that it had controlled most of the continent for 70 years. Did British monopolies not think that Africa was a growth area, he asked? Were there political risks? Were profits enough? Were joint ventures desirable? Did they want tax and other concessions as inducements to future investment?

To the first question, their response was that there were doubts as to the future prospects of the region, but that the continuance of the common market would make growth prospects 'brighter' if communications within and between the three territories were improved.[28] Many regarded the area as a growth area for particular products and markets, provided the political climate was favourable.[29]

On the issue of the political climate, the monopolies were agreed that they lacked confidence in the stability of the region overall. Although conditions for stability in Uganda and Kenya were seen as generally favourable, 'they were more hesitant over Tanzania, largely because of doubts of Zanzibar's attitude towards private investment';[30] i.e. after the political changes there in 1964. Morgan summarized: 'The recent taking over of a further batch of minor industries by the Government of Zanzibar indicates that the political threats to private investment remain.'[31] Zanzibar, nevertheless, was taken to be exceptional in the area. Although prospects for a political federation had faded, it was hoped that the Kampala Agreement would hold good and the East African Common Services Organization would continue.

On the question of whether profits were high enough, most of the mono-polies said that political risks tended to cancel out the wish to invest, despite the high profit rates; the risk demanded much higher profits. Generally, they expected returns of 20 to 25% on the basis of investments maturing in less than three years.[32] On the question of joint ventures, many of the mono-polies still emphasized the danger of expropriation, but some expressed willingness to partner with local capital – preferably private, but some were prepared to work with the state if left with no choice.

As regards tax incentives and protection, over half of the monopolies expected tax and other concessions. The others felt that 'help in earning profits' was more important than concessions. Almost all the monopolies mentioned tax holidays, duty-free importation of machinery and raw mater-ials, and a 'temporary local monopoly and freedom of movement of funds' as essential incentives.[33] Almost all of them emphasized the need for an East African common market.

These expectations of British finance capital in the changed situation are important, for they reflected the general expectations of multilateral finance capital, and constituted the basis of the neo-colonial policies which were worked out by the three neo-colonial states in the period 1964–5 as prerequisites to 'attract foreign investment'. Indeed, all three development plans immediately after independence emphasized the role of foreign capital in their projects.[34] This is partly due to the fact that investment in the region had actually declined drastically in the period before the plans.[35]

It is thus hardly surprising that all the plans emphasized the expansion of export crops to augment foreign exchange earnings, in part to pay for growing imports related to this investment, as Seidman has noted.[36] Such reliance on foreign sources of financing had as its corollary the framing of policies favourable to foreign capital. All three countries passed in their legislatures a Foreign Investment Protection Act which guaranteed *inter alia* security for such investments with the further promise that, should expropriations become necessary in the public interest, full or adequate compensation would be paid promptly. Uganda and Tanganyika also provided an Industrial Charter which gave further guarantees, but since these guarantees had in fact been negotiated and inserted in the Independence Constitutions (except Tanganyika's) the charters merely reconfirmed these constitutional provisions.

Furthermore, under the East African Income Tax (Management) Act of 1958, all three countries granted incentives in the form of an 'investment deduction' of 20% in respect of industrial machinery and buildings, and 'annual deductions' which allowed 120% of any such investment to be written off. The East African Customs Tariff (Management) Act of 1958 also granted tariff protection to import-substitution industries, as well as giving waivers to these monopolies of any future duties on the importation of raw materials and the duty-free importation of machinery. Refund of any duties paid was also promised, if approved by the East African Tariff Committee. Remissions of customs duty were also granted in order to give 'temporary local monopoly' to those monopolies 'who would otherwise be unable to achieve a competitive position'.[37]

This policy was pursued in spite of the fact noted by Morgan that 'many manufacturers deferred setting up factories overseas until they were about to lose a market in a territory and then they were prepared to manufacture locally at increased cost and lower profit margins than they would at home'.[38] Indeed, as we shall see later, most import-substitution industry in Tanganyika and Uganda came into this category.(This is true of most of Africa.)[39]

In addition to tariff protection, there were additional incentive mechanisms for the monopoly investors. Under the External Trade Acts, orders were made by Ministers prohibiting the importation of certain goods on grounds of balance of payments difficulties. Since no licence could be issued where products were locally produced or where those produced were substitutable, this mechanism offered almost 100% protection to certain monopoly-initiated industries. Then there was the transfer tax provision of the Treaty for East African Co-operation of 1967, under which a tax was imposed on goods originating from members of the common market in order to protect 'infant industries' producing goods similar to those imported or where they were reasonably expected to be produced within three months in the importing and hence tax-imposing state. Kenya and Uganda also signed the World Bank-sponsored International Convention on the Settlement of Investment Disputes Between States and Nationals of Other States, whereby disputes between those states and the monopolies could go to arbitration under World Bank chairmanship.

As if all these monopoly privileges were not adequate, the three states also entered into a number of separate bilateral investment guarantee treaties with West Germany, the U.S. and Switzerland under which further guarantees were given. In addition, all three countries granted lower rates and charges on water, electricity and railway freight, as well as freely constructing access-roads and subsidized railway sidings for industry. At the same time, the three countries imposed trade union laws which stringently restricted wage increases and controlled labour organization and strike action. All these tools were of great assistance in assuring the dominance of international finance capital. In the following chapters we will now discuss each of the three countries' economies separately.

References

1. D.W. Nabudere, *The Political Economy of Imperialism* (London/Dar es Salaam, Zed Press, 1977), p. vii.
2. *Ibid.*, pp. 144–5.
3. R. Gardner, *Sterling-Dollar Diplomacy* (New York, McGraw-Hill, 1969), pp. 17–18.
4. W.A. Dymsza, *The Multinational Corporate Strategy* (New York, McGraw Hill, 1972), pp. 195–6.
5. *Ibid.*, p. 12.
6. Quoted in B. Nissen and U. Weismann, *The Trojan Horse* (New York, Ramparts Press, 1974), p. 45.
7. See footnotes 8, 9 and 10 below for reference.
8. I.B.R.D., *The Economic Development of Tanganyika* (Baltimore, Johns Hopkins, 1961), pp. 33, 238–9.
9. I.B.R.D., *The Economic Development of Uganda* (Baltimore, Johns Hopkins, 1962), pp. 89–95.
10. I.B.R.D,, *The Economic Development of Kenya* (Baltimore, Johns Hopkins, 1963), pp. vii–viii.
11. I.B.R.D., *Tanganyika, op. cit.*, pp. 6, 130–1.
12. *Ibid.*, pp. 229–33.
13. *Ibid.*, p. 234.
14. *Ibid.*, pp. 241–3.
15. *Ibid.*, p. vii.
16. I.B.R.D., *Uganda, op. cit.*, pp. 50–2, 96–257.
17. *Ibid.*, p. 272.
18. *Ibid.*, pp. 293–4.
19. *Ibid.*, pp. 296–7.

20. I.B.R.D., *Kenya, op. cit.,* p. vii.
21. *Ibid.,* pp. 301–2, 63–142.
22. *Ibid.,* p. 306.
23. *Ibid.*
24. U.S.A.I.D., *Tanganyika Five Year Industrial Plan* (Washington, D.C., 1964).
25. *Ibid.,* p. 63.
26. *Ibid.,* p. 31.
27. D.J. Morgan, *British Private Investment in East Africa* (London, O.D.I., 1965).
28. *Ibid.,* pp. 24, 43.
29. *Ibid.,* pp. 16–17, 24.
30. *Ibid.,* p. 44.
31. *Ibid.,* p. 44.
32. *Ibid.,* pp. 15, 19.
33. *Ibid.,* pp. 15, 21.
34. P.G. Clark, *Development Planning in East Africa* (Nairobi, East Africa Publishing House, 1965), pp. 51–2; see also B. van Arkadie, 'Private Foreign Investment: Some Limitations' in P.A. Thomas, *Private Enterprise and the East African Company* (Dar es Salaam, Tanzania Publishing House, 1967), p. 157.
35. Clark, *op. cit.,* p. 18.
36. A.W. Seidman, 'Some Comments on Planning in East Africa' in J. Saul and L. Cliffe (eds.), *Socialism in Tanzania* (Nairobi, East Africa Publishing House, 1972), Vol. II, p. 82.
37. W. Kalema, 'Private Enterprise in Uganda' in Thomas, *op. cit.,* p. 175.
38. Morgan, *op. cit.,* p. 47.
39. A. Seidmann and R. Greene, *Unity of Poverty: The Economics of Pan-Africanism* (London, Penguin, 1968), p. 99.

7. The Tanzanian Neo-Colonial Economy

As we noted in Chapter Two, at the beginning of independence Tanzania had very little British or other foreign investment; and what little foreign capital had been generated locally towards the end of the colonial era was now going elsewhere.[1] This was happening in other parts of East Africa of course, but particularly in Tanzania. In 1964 alone expatriate purchase of foreign securities amounted to £8,763,000, as compared to £5,157,000 in 1963 and £4,300,000 in 1962; this represented a considerable shift of private capital. In 1964 there was another 'unidentified outflow' of £6,587,000, while monetary reserves rose by only £3,004,000. As Yaffey has observed:

> Thus, of the £14 million increase in foreign exchange receipts, £3 million went into official reserves, a little over £1 million went into increased merchandise imports, and most of the remainder went into capital outflow, £5 million of it identified, and a large unidentified outflow which may be presumed to consist mainly of private capital outflow.[2]

He adds that further capital outflow was 'concealed in higher import prices' and in 'higher profit remittances'.

In these circumstances, and given the economic weakness of the local bourgeoisie, it can be understood why the new Tanzanian Government was held by the throat and had to accept the terms demanded by international capital. The belief that Tanzania could go forward only on the basis of attracting international capital seemed almost natural. As Rweyemamu has noted, 'It was assumed that foreign private capital would easily flow into Tanzania if favourable conditions, such as were suggested by the World Bank Report and the Arthur D. Little Report, were created.'[3] That was certainly true of industrialization.

In agriculture and other government activities, it was also believed that official 'aid' would be easily found if stability was maintained. For instance, the shortfall in the government budget in the fiscal year 1961/62, was, in the 1962–63 budget, thought to be remediable by the new finance which would soon flow in from all sources. Clark has noted:

In his budget speech, the Minister of Finance discussed in a quite illuminating way the financial problems involved in shifting from complete reliance on U.K. financing, provided largely on a programme basis and often after expenditure had been initiated, to a system of foreign aid from many sources, largely on a project basis and with the necessity of complete agreement before initiating expenditure.[4]

In return, of course, the new multilateral system quite clearly imposed a new discipline on Tanzania suited to the multilateral integration of the economy with many imperialist state and private monopolies. In this system the foreign investor had to agree to each project before the money could be released. This over-reliance on external multilateral and bilateral financing was reflected in the 79% external financing for the Plan[5] for the period 1961 to 1964. In the event, external sourcing only provided 73% which meant that Tanzania had to find local finance to meet the shortfall by increasing the allocation of tax revenue from £1 million to £3 million.[6] This nevertheless indicated a relatively easy access to foreign finance, reflected in the further enthusiasm for it shown in the next 'comprehensive plan'.

The First Five Year Plan

The First Five Year Plan (F.F.Y.P.), which came into force in 1964, was heralded as a new approach to development planning.[7] Its four main objectives were achieving a growth rate of 6.7%; raising *per capita* incomes from £19.6 to £45 by 1980; training local manpower to 'self-sufficiency' by the same date; and raising life expectancy from 35–40 to 50 years. These objectives were based on the hope that foreign capital would contribute at least 18% of the total capital requirements of the Shs. 4,920 million planned expenditure, of which 53% was to come from the public sector and the remainder from the private sector. Investments in agriculture were based on the expectation that production of cash crops for export would earn the country adequate foreign exchange resources for its development and that, through this type of trade, the 'engine of growth' of the country would be assured.[8]

It was on this false assumption that the whole rural strategy, the 'transformation approach', was based. The Village Settlement Schemes envisaged under the F.F.Y.P. all depended on the injection of foreign capital. Although it was realized that this strategy would take time to mature, it was argued that the schemes would 'bring about a relatively abrupt transition of the people concerned to modern techniques with regard to land use, land tenure and patterns of agricultural production, and economic attitudes'. It was further believed that the settlement villages could 'also be relied upon in the future to relieve incipient land hunger and population pressure in certain areas'.[9] Each scheme was to involve 250 individual family farms and was to cost £150,000 per settlement, 60 of which were to be embarked on in the plan period.

In the area of manufacturing, private investment was expected to play a leading role under the inducement of the various incentives already mentioned. Government involvement would be limited to providing local finance and carrying out surveys and studies of projects of interest to private investment. In the planned development, emphasis was to be placed on import substitution in manufacturing.

But, in the event, international finance capital did not come up to expectations and in the first four years of the plan the government was forced to raise 60% of the finance from local sources. A detailed account of the reasons for this will be given later, but, in general, government officials noted that foreign investors and donors were balking at the stage of approving the projects which the plan had projected. Furthermore, it turned out that the monopolies expected most of the capital to be raised locally and insisted that their own capital be tied to their imports, all of which had to be inserted into negotiated agreements.[10]

The result was that the settlement schemes turned out to be extremely costly, both in terms of local capital as well as reluctant foreign capital. Although export crop production did increase, this was mainly from the traditional small-holding peasant sector and not from the new and larger settlement villages. Indeed, it was noted that, as far as agriculture was concerned, it was precisely where reliance on foreign capital had been least that performance had been more than satisfactory.[11] Production of cash crops like cotton, coffee, sugar and cashew nuts had increased 'impressively' in the plan period, with 'greater diversification of crops and an increase in productivity'. In the future, it now appeared, 'the agricultural sector could be relied upon to maintain a steady growth rate'.[12]

Despite this apparent good news for the countryside, the rural incomes of the peasantry fell in the same period, with the poor peasant getting the worst deal. This is not to be attributed to the worsening of the terms of trade and the 'pattern of surplus utilization'[13] but to the whole system of international exploitation based on the export of capital (tied to local capital) which was still being imposed on Tanzania. This was, of course, partly reflected in declining terms of trade between agricultural products and manufactured goods in general, but this was not itself the real exploitation. The real exploitation has to be noted at the level of wages and the surplus value extracted (including taxes by the neo-colonial state 'for national development') by the monopolies incorporated unrecompensed into the product. As it was, the level of prices fell and the neo-colonial state found it increasingly difficult to see any 'engine of growth' in this trade. But, given no option by the objective situation, it continued the pattern of agricultural production in the 'hope' that some day things might change.

In the field of manufacturing, beginning in 1961 the government worked out an elaborate tariff protection scheme to be extended to investors in import-substitution industries with a warning to the Kenya-based companies that, unless they invested in Tanzania to produce locally, they would lose their markets. And, since they lost nothing by moving in to take advantage of the protection, many did so. Rweyemamu has demonstrated that most, if not all, of the import substitution industrialization that took place in this period in Tanzania was 'conditional on granting the industrialists adequate tariff protection'.[14] He indicates that the initiative did not actually lie with the government but with the investors:

> Indeed, from accounts given by the officials of the Ministry who deal with these issues, the initiative originates with the potential investors who submit a request for a tariff increase (and perhaps also for a duty relief on imported raw materials, component parts or machinery), accompanied by an investment proposal and a set of cost estimates.[15]

Due to the state officials' 'ignorance' of the cost estimates, Rweyemamu adds, the investor invariably managed to obtain more than 'sufficient' protection, and hence could keep away rivals in the same field. But this was by the way. Dudley Kessel's[16] study of 'effective protection' in Tanzania revealed that even the *normal* tariff protection granted in the country was extremely misleading in that it actually gave the investor much more effective protection than envisaged under the tariff of 100% and more in the tobacco, matches and beer industries. This further revealed a tendency for consumer goods industries, which were in fact being encouraged, particularly those with a luxury bias, to be 'heavily protected'.[17]

This 'protection' had serious implications for discussions about the advantages of import substitution and is very telling for the theoretical and general observations made in the previous chapter about monopolistic competition under the new conditions prevailing under multilateral imperialism. For, as Rweyemamu observes, such protection not only secures the investor in those products but it also shields that investing monopoly 'to a substantial degree from [the] technically more advanced varieties or otherwise superior articles which, in the absence of fiscal discrimination, might pre-empt the market'.[18]

In other words, no technological advantage at all was secured by a country extending such protection to the monopoly; on the contrary, a monopoly with no particular technological advantage over others, and indeed possibly even more backward competitively, was being protected against other monopolies which might otherwise have an advantage over it. But this had to be so at a time when most technology in mass-produced goods on a world scale (many of them 'luxuries' in East Africa) was highly standardized. In such monopolistic competitive conditions, the investor would have to seek protection as the major component of competitive advantage, and this is what was happening in Tanzania as elsewhere in East Africa.

This had not been the case in the previous period, as Rweyemamu notes, in terms of the small market share of overseas (i.e. British) suppliers and the effect of technical skill barriers 'sufficiently high' in those (bilateral) conditions to exclude deploying merchant firms importing those products. In such a situation 'import substitution may long be delayed because the interests of no single firm are materially jeopardized'.[19] But, put in its historical context and the context of political economy, such development explains why import substitution in Tanzania was 'delayed'. Thus, whereas a certain 'technological threshhold' had been achieved in Tanzania in the period under consideration, the lag in import-substitution industrialization was created by the lack of competition dictated by British monopoly capital. In the textile industry, in particular, British capital discouraged any competition in East Africa, and in fact went as far as excluding the Japanese effort to build a factory there. When this monopoly was removed by the change in the balance of forces in the 1950s, the British merchant houses — on the one hand strengthened by the new multilateral discipline stipulated under G.A.T.T. and the I.M.F., and on the other hand threatened by the possibility of losing their safe markets — engaged in the import substitution strategy in East Africa under industrial licensing. In Uganda, for instance, more cotton was grown, a textile factory was built, and, as we will shortly see, the same combination of forces also compelled similar moves in Tanzania, resulting in 'a sudden cluster of investment'.[20]

Just as monopoly capitalism had been forced by Japanese competition to permit the Tanganyika Cordage Company to set up import-substitute industry in the late 1930s, despite earlier opposition to it,[21] now, under the open neo-colonial conditions, it was equally forced into import substitution as a way of defending markets. Between 1961 and 1968 no fewer than five textile industries were established in Tanzania, as were a number of other manufacturing industries such as plywood, sisal twine, maize flour, cement and blankets. This development was further confirmed institutionally by the fact that most of this import substitution was undertaken by former importing houses, mainly already located in Tanzania. It was Tanzania's pressure to create industrial investment which led to the Kampala Agreement in 1964 (amended in 1965) and the imposition of import restrictions and quotas against Kenyan-produced goods. The outcome was 'a burst of industrial investment in Tanzania, which almost equalled the country's whole previous manufacturing sector for consumer goods'.[22]

This push for development was made possible by British importers' fears of losing the market to the new monopolies. No longer were arguments for an East African market being heard; all the theorizing hitherto uttered about the 'size of the market' was jettisoned. So long as these monopolies — now coerced by the sheer force of monopolistic competition to *transnationalize* their production — operated in this way and were assisted by the protection of the neo-colonial state structure, this was adequate integration at the level of international production and the market. What was happening was that a further concentration of production on a world scale was being forced on the more backward British monopolies by other European, U.S. and Japanese monopolies.

The operation of these forces can be seen very vividly in the activities of the British monopoly, Unilever,[23] or rather its local East African subsidiary, Gailey and Roberts, which was actively involved in textile import substitution in Tanzania. In 1961 only one textile factory existed in the country. With independence and the possible loss of the market, within six years many new plants were established by existing importers. The first of these, Tasini Textiles, was set up by established importers, Smith and Mackenzie and Co. and Dalgety and Co., together with a Dutch textile consortium and a local co-operative and government finance corporation partly owned by the Dutch Government.[24] The new competition was obviously forcing a merger of interests. The case of the Mwanza Textile Mill also shows such a merger of interests, this time connected specifically with the way in which inter-European competition[25] forced outmoded machinery into relatively backward markets.[26] In the case of MWATEX the 20% participation by Amenital Holding Registered Trust was motivated by the need to get rid of the old machinery of an associate, Societe-Alsacienne des Constructions Mecaniques de Mulhause, reinforced by the fact that the financing of the purchase of the machinery was handled by the supplier's credit of Shs. 60 million, repayable over eight years at an interest rate of 5.7% per annum. This participation gave the factory management to Sodefra Maurer Textiles of Geneva, representatives of Amenital, which brought an interesting web of monopolistic tie-ups involving paying Sodefra Shs. 3.5 million as a fee for testing and preparing an engineering report in another industry for a sisal pulp project of the National Development Corporation, as well as a management contract for the Mwanza Hotel.[27] No wonder a special investment guarantee treaty with Switzerland had to be signed to protect further the interests of this new Swiss monopoly in Tanzania!

Kilimanjaro Textiles, set up in 1967, was another good example of the criss-crossing of the new monopoly interests in East Africa, with West German monopolies both defending the earlier market of their importing firm Jos Hansen and Söhne and co-operating with British state capital in the same venture. The British textile management monopoly, Calico, was also involved in setting up a new plant. Local investment, too, found its way into this criss-crossing of joint venture investments with outside monopolies.[28]

The threat that new monopoly capital would enter the Tanzanian investment field as a result of the new developments is also noted by Rweyemamu with respect to radio manufacturing. Philips Industries, which had a 90% monopoly of the market in imports between 1958 and 1962, was forced to import substitute in order to defend its share of the market when the Japanese monopoly Matsushita Electric Co. overtook it, increasing its share of the market from 1.4% in 1958 to 68% by 1962. As a result of this competition Philips' share had fallen to 21% in 1964. The Kampala Agreement of 1964, which allocated the radio industry to Tanzania, merely accelerated an already foregone decision by Philips to import substitute. With the 50% tariff protection granted to Philips, an apparently inefficient producer which had demonstrably failed to hold the market was given a 'temporary local monopoly' to dominate the market at monopoly prices. Matsushita, thus thrown out of the market, proceeded to set up a battery factory in Dar es Salaam where it obtained its own 'temporary local monopoly' and its own tariff protection.

Rweyemamu gives the example of oil refining to demonstrate this competition in a potentially new market. An Italian oil monopoly had built a refinery at Mombasa, and the prospect of a pipeline to Zambia from Tanzania and a possible refinery there put the Italian company in a 'strong competitive position' with the tariff protection granted to it to establish a similar refinery with the Tanzania Government in Dar es Salaam.

Other monopolistic considerations, such as participation in the export market (meat canning, pyrethrum extract, wattle extract, cashew nut processing, cordage, rope and twine, coffee and tea, and diamonds) also contributed to tariff-protected industrialization in Tanzania in this period and brought in a new type of investor from many countries, together with a few local investors. The need to dispose of machinery by an Italian monopoly, for example, seems to have played a part in establishing cashew nut investment,[29] the loss of which brought in a Japanese monopoly to replace the Italian one.

All this information is detailed here in order to raise the problems caused by the failure of regional economic integration to consolidate. (This will be further examined in the next chapters and in Vol. 2.) It also will help us to discuss the material on Uganda and Kenya in the same period, since all these investment activities were highly interconnected not only on a world scale but in East Africa as well, where the battles over particular markets and investment outlets were being fought out in a new environment.

The Role of the Neo-Colonial State

Despite this spate of investment activity in Tanzania, relatively little private capital came in to assist in import substitution. Although by 1968 manufacturing had achieved an 'extremely high' growth rate of 12 to 13% in terms of value added, it nevertheless did not reach the 'somewhat exaggerated target set in the plan'.[30] Whereas it had been expected that external financing would provide 78% of the plan's financial requirements, in fact less than 40% was forthcoming. In manufacturing, in particular, where 60% of the investment was expected to come from foreign-owned reinvestment of profits earned by existing firms, the expansion in investment was very 'sluggish', rising at only 0.8% per annum.[31]

As we have already observed, there was a very large outflow (perhaps one third of the total capital formation in the private sector) in 1964, partly attributable to the army mutiny, the changes in Zanzibar and Kenya's independence. The net outflow of Shs. 279 million of private capital in the early stages of the First Five Year Plan led to the imposition of exchange control measures within the Sterling Area in 1965 to arrest the overflow. In late 1965 there was a net inflow of Shs. 21 million and in 1966 Shs. 90 million.[32] But this did not improve the position as regards private capital investment. On the contrary, short-term capital showed a net outflow of

Shs. 14 million in these years. Despite the strengthening brought about by the net inflow of long-term capital, there was still an overall private capital outflow in 1965 of Shs. 11 million. The situation was saved only by substantial borrowing and grants, both long term and short term, on the public sector capital account, which together brought in a total of Shs. 63 million, 'which [went] half-way to offsetting the fall in exports'.[33]

Thus, by 1967, even before the Arusha Declaration, the state was becoming the major factor in investment and production in the entire Tanzanian economy.[34] As Yaffey has correctly pointed out:

> Private capital, having trickled in (partly in the form of settlers' savings) in the past, and having established a considerable annual outflow of investment income, registered a net outflow in the early independence years, thereby shifting the emphasis to public capital, so that the present predominance of the public sector — quite aside from domestic reasons — became an economic necessity. The private outflow was reversed in 1965 by exchange control measures, but still showed signs of weakness [late 1966] and by no reckoning could it be expected to show substantial annual growth at the rate necessary to offset the negative balance of payments effects of its own amortization. A path of development of the early Latin American type is therefore out of the question. With the growth of official capital inflow and donations, the Government has achieved an increasing measure of control over the economy.[35]

Those, like Shivji, who have tried to trace the rise of a 'new ruling class' of the 'bureaucratic bourgeoisie' in Tanzania back to the weakness of the petty bourgeoisie and the weak kulak class in the countryside,[36] should note that it was the lack of inflow of private capital, and the tendency of existing capital to withdraw, that increasingly pushed the state to take control of the economy, not for itself, as has been suggested, but for international capital. The lack of a national bourgeoisie, a fact that characterizes all the neo-colonies, though not all taking the same path as Tanzania, is of course an important factor, but its very non-existence has to be explained as a historically determined factor.

It is for this reason that, despite the very limited private capital in the economy, the industrial development that took place in Tanzania was financed by the state-controlled finance corporations who lent capital to private industry. The setting up of the N.D.C., the Tanzania Development Finance Company (T.D.F.L.) (which was equally shared by the Governments of Tanzania, West Germany, the Netherlands and the U.K.), as well as other financial institutions (established on the recommendation of the World Bank) all went to strengthen industry of the type we have indicated.

All this contributed to further entrenching the state's role in the economy, as increasingly one of intermediary for international finance capital, and thus helping to reorient the economy in a new type of integration under multilateral imperialism. The interruption in the flow of capital also took place on occasion in the public sector, despite its growing importance. President Nyerere himself explained[37] that aid which had been promised by Germany, the U.S. and the U.K. had not arrived for various political reasons connected with Tanzania's efforts to consolidate her national independence.

Thus the situation in 1967 consisted of a net outflow of private capital; state capital playing an increasingly crucial role in attracting limited amounts of official aid but relying more and more on internal mobilization to implement the F.F.Y.P.; industry playing only a minor role in the gross domestic product despite its rapid expansion; and agriculture expanding more than expected but out of local funds earned from exports and other internal sources. No wonder it appeared to the government, and particularly to the democratic petty bourgeoisie in TANU, that, if Tanzania was to develop its national economy, it had to rely on its own effort rather than on foreign aid. It is for this reason that the Arusha Declaration emphasized self-reliance and possibilities of a non-monetary sector. It condemned those who saw money as the only means to future development:

> It is stupid to rely on money as the major instrument of development when we know only too well that our country is poor. It is equally stupid, indeed it is even more stupid, for us to imagine that we shall rid ourselves of our poverty through foreign assistance rather than our own financial resources.[38]

It was stupid, the Declaration continued, for two reasons: first, money would not be forthcoming from these sources, and second, even if it were available in adequate amounts, it would compromise Tanzania's independence. It continued, 'Independence means self reliance . . . . To burden the people with big loans, the repayment of which will be beyond their means, is not only not to help them but to make them suffer.'[39] Democratic sentiments aside, the Declaration was really expressing disillusion with miscalculated expectations. It is clear that no such declaration would have been made had the expected funds flowed in. Furthermore, however idealistically invoked, its emphasis on a strong state role itself served in producing, mobilizing, and investing resources for application by such international finance capital as continued to trickle in.

The new policies which were carried out in the wake of the Declaration were fivefold: self-reliance, rural development, more equitable distribution, national economic control and socialism. Self-reliance implied not the total rejection of all aid but an increasing dependence on local effort and resources. Emphasis on rural development was the recognition of its role in the previous plan and the realization that 90% of the population lived and worked in the villages. It was this population which had to be mobilized if the next plan was to succeed. As for national economic control, it was a necessary concomitant of the dominant role of the state in the economy and this, according to the Declaration, was necessary since it was the only institution

that could mobilize and allocate resources and effort 'equitably'. And socialism was itself a prerequisite of equity for all those on whom the development
effort depended.

Some of these policies had in fact already been implemented as the crisis
of exploitation engulfed the country.[40] But the nationalization of banks,
insurance companies, industries, trading concerns, the sisal industry and, in
1971, buildings, was seen as implementing the policy of *Ujamaa* and self-
reliance.[41] The take-over of banks and insurance companies as well as trading
concerns enabled a large mobilization of resources formerly repatriated as
profits by private capital.

However, nationalized industries continued to be run by the former investing monopolies on the basis of management agreements. These nationalization measures did not in any way affect private property relations in the
country, and, as long as the characteristic neo-colonial export-import
orientation continued, there was no change in the production pattern. All
the nationalized industries were by law to continue to operate on the 'best
commercial principles'. Through the good offices of the World Bank, the
I.M.F., GATT and other international institutions, the imperialist monopolies
continued to oversee and supervise the economy. With a confident role
laid out for the state, the 1967-68 budget actually stepped up reliance on
foreign aid to £12 million, which marked what De La Rue saw as a 'turning
point', in that 'for the first time Tanzania had regained the 1961-62 level of
foreign loans and grants received after a 50% fall in 1963-64 and a rather
sluggish recovery since'.[42]

The Second Five Year Plan

The Second Five Year Plan (S.F.Y.P.), which came into force in 1969,
proposed that government investment should double to Shs. 2,750 million
(as against Shs. 1,322 million in the F.F.Y.P.), while private investment was
relegated to a minor role. But the government still relied for 45% of its
financial needs on external sources, more than was achieved in the F.F.Y.P.
period.

The emphasis on rural development consisted in the new policy of *Ujamaa*
villages, as opposed to the settlement villages of the F.F.Y.P. A third of all
funds were to be spent on agricultural production in a 'frontal of broadly
based transformation approach', involving mobilization and participation.
The approach to industry which was to account for only 14% of investment
was one of caution. Although the F.F.Y.P. had recognized that in the long
run economic development required the creation of an industrial base, yet
'for the present', it was pointed out, the 'foundation of socialism [had to]
be built on the rural sector'. By 1973 this plan was having its own problems.
Foreign capital continued to flow in in the form of official or multilateral
loans, and the World Bank was becoming the largest exporter of capital to
Tanzania. The Arusha Declaration's rural strategy, based on voluntary entry

into collective villages, was being replaced by a policy of coercion. The reality of neo-colonial exploitation was beginning to tell and was rapidly sweeping away the illusions that an egalitarian society could be created without smashing the exploitative relationships based on capitalist production in the interests of international finance capital. It was no problem for this capital to go on tapping the resources now being mobilized in the countryside for its own needs.

Under these conditions it was impossible to secure the balanced rural development that could equitably distribute incomes among the population. To cap this, in the five years (1968–73) agricultural production increased at 2.49% annually but this was slower than in the F.F.Y.P. period, and could not keep pace with the population increase of 2.7%. Investment in agriculture had slowed down, and the country therefore had to spend a further Shs. 1.2 billion to import food — a development much exacerbated by the oil crisis. This stagnation in food production implied that a new orientation was required; by this time, the government was abandoning its rural strategy of collective *Ujamaa* villages in favour of 'development villages' based on individual holdings into which the World Bank was pumping money to produce tobacco and other cash crops.[43]

In the field of food production, a new strategy, based on a combination of 'Tanzanian land/labour with Arab money and American technology', was implemented in the capital-intensive National Maize Project. This represented such a shift in the Arusha Declaration's emphasis on self-reliance,[44] (since it was making the peasants increasingly dependent on imported capital in-puts) that President Nyerere himself wondered whether it had anything in common with declared policy.[45] The rural economy was being drawn back to the old strategy of supporting the 'progressive farmer' with credits, price incentives and new techniques. A new National Agricultural Development Project was being worked out to replace the earlier broad-based strategies of the Arusha Declaration. By 1980 the policy had led to a decrease in food production and an emphasis on cash crop production.

In the field of manufacturing, although the private sector still accounted for the largest number of registered companies — 430 establishments employing 10 or more people, as against 70 parastatals, the latter accounted for 75% of the value added and 90% of new capital formation. The main sources of capital for financing new industries and expanding old ones, despite the Declaration, were foreign, with local and state capital playing only a subsidiary role. The Tanzania Investment Bank (T.I.B.) became the main financier of many industries, supported by the T.I.D.B. and the East African Development Bank (E.A.D.B.). All foreign loans and equity contributions were channelled through the Treasury and the Bank of Tanzania.

Despite the call for self-reliance the external debt has built up quickly since 1971. From Shs. 747.2 million in 1967, it rose to Shs. 1,292 million by the end of 1971. And as of March 1978 the external debt stood at an incredible Shs. 13,168,771,524, over ten times greater than the 1971 figure. The Minister revealed that this debt was raised from 'international organizations and friendly countries'.[46]

By 1973 the period of over-protected import substitution was also coming to an end. Productivity under the Second Plan had been low due to various factors and the 'top-heavy' parastatal arrangement in industry — with 11 holding parastatals and 70 operative ones — created a serious labour shortage. The export markets within the East African common market before its break-up were beginning to stagnate as each country produced for its own market. Thus, international finance capital, through the agency of the state, had continued its grip on the economy of Tanzania under new conditions of multilateral monopolistic competition. Agriculture and industry served the interests of the imperialist monopolies. President Nyerere himself came near to accepting this dominance when speaking at Ibadan University:

> Neo-colonialism is a very real, and very severe, limitation on national sovereignty. The total amount of credit and its distribution to different sectors of the economy, for example, is determined by the banking system. The persons or groups who control the banks, therefore, have a very fundamental — almost a deciding — effect at two points. The first is on the level of current economic activity in a money economy; the second is on the comparative advantage of, say, peasant agriculture as against estate agriculture, or agriculture in general as against the development of local industry or trade. The local agents of foreign banks may well be willing to co-operate with the national government's priorities; but in the last resort their loyalty is, and must be, to their overseas employers. In case of disputes at the top policy level, the government will not be able to enforce its decisions. It may be able to stop things; it will not be able to start things. Matters of vital interest to our development are thus determined externally, without any consideration being given to our interests.[47]

References

1. J. Loxley, 'Structural Change in the Monetary System of Tanzania' in J. Saul and L. Cliffe (eds.), *Socialism in Tanzania*, Vol. II (Nairobi, East Africa Publishing House, 1972), p. 104.
2. M.J.F. Yaffey, *Balance of Payments Problems of a Developing Country: Tanzania* (Munich, Welt Forum Verlag, 1968), p. 73.
3. J.F. Rweyemamu, *Underdevelopment and Industrialization in Tanzania: A Study of Perverse Capitalist Industrial Development* (London/Nairobi, Oxford University Press, 1973), p. 39.
4. P.G. Clark, *Development Planning in East Africa* (Nairobi, East Africa Publishing House, 1965), p. 50.
5. A term used by Clark to distinguish the early post-colonial plans from the 'comprehensive' New Plans which began around 1965–6.
6. Clark, *op. cit.,* p. 52.

7. Brian van Arkadie, *Planning in Tanzania* in Saul and Cliffe, *op. cit.*, Vol. II, p. 25.
8. Rweyemamu, *op. cit.*, p. 40.
9. *First Five Year Plan* (1964–69), Vol. I, p. 21.
10. Arkadie, *op. cit.*, p. 25.
11. B. Ngotyana, 'The Strategy of Rural Development' in Saul and Cliffe, *op. cit.*
12. *Ibid.*, p. 125.
13. Rweyemamu, *op. cit.*, pp. 54–6.
14. *Ibid.*, p. 56.
15. *Ibid.*, p. 130.
16. *Ibid.*, pp. 130–1.
17. D. Kessel, 'Effective Protection in Tanzania', ERB Paper 67.8 (mimeo) and *East African Economic Review*, June 1968.
18. Rweyemamu, *op. cit.*, pp. 133-5.
19. *Ibid.*, p. 100.
20. *Ibid.*, pp. 100-1.
21. *Ibid.*, p. 122.
22. E.A. Brett, *Colonialism and Underdevelopment in East Africa* (London, Heinemann, 1973), p. 279.
23. A. Seidmann and R. Green, *Unity or Poverty: The Economics of Pan-Africanism* (London, Penguin, 1968), p. 145.
24. *Ibid.*, pp. 109-11.
25. Rweyemamu, *op. cit.*, p. 123.
26. O.E.C.D., *Modern Cotton Industry, A Capital Intensive Industry* (Paris, O.E.C.D., 1961), p. 95.
27. H. Helmschrott, 'Structure and Growth of the East African Industry' in Zajadaczp, (ed.), *Studies in Production and Trade in East Africa* (Munich, Welt Forum Verlag, 1970), pp. 38-9.
28. Rweyemamu, *op. cit.*, pp. 123-4.
29. For an excellent account of this investment activity see *ibid.*, p. 124.
30. *Ibid.*, p. 129.
31. Arkadie, *op. cit.*, pp. 29-30.
32. Rweyemamu, *op. cit.*, p. 52.
33. Yaffey, *op. cit.*, pp. 33, 81-2.
34. *Ibid.*, p. 82.
35. Tanzania Government, *Background to the Budget 1965-1966* (Dar es Salaam, Government Printer).
36. Yaffey, *op. cit.*, pp. 98-9.
37. I. Shivji, *Class Struggles in Tanzania* (Dar es Salaam, Heinemann/ Tanzania Publishing House, 1975).
38. J. Nyerere, 'Principles and Development' in J. Nyerere, *Freedom and Socialism* (London, Oxford University Press, 1968).
39. J. Nyerere, 'The Arusha Declaration' in *ibid.*, pp. 238-9.
40. *Ibid.*, p. 240.
41. Andre de la Rue, 'Ujamaa on the March' in Saul and Cliffe, *op. cit.*, Vol. II, pp. 44-52.
42. For details of these nationalizations see *Background to the Budget 1967-68* and Rweyemamu, *op. cit.*, pp. 57-74., de la Rue, *op. cit.*, p. 49.

43. D.W. Nabudere, *Essays in the Theory and Practice of Imperialism* (London/D.S.M., Onyx Press/Tanzania Publishing House, 1978).
44. Y. Tandon, 'The Socio-Economic Implications of the Transfer of Maize Tecynology in Tanzania', (Dar es Salaam, mimeo, 1978).
45. *Daily News*, 18 December 1978.
46. *Daily News*, 25 September 1978.
47. J.K. Nyerere, 'Process of Liberation', *Daily News*, 18 November 1976.

8. The Ugandan Neo-Colonial Economy

The multilateral integration of the Ugandan economy into international corporate monopolies proceeded on similar lines to Tanzania. Indeed, all three countries arranged similar incentives and protection for the monopolies to attract investment. These parallel arrangements were worked out and handed over to the new neo-colonial states by the World Bank in response to their new status as neo-colonial nation-states. Thus the divergent economic policies these countries began to pursue to attract the monopolies to their territories was a natural line to pursue and was consistent with the new monopolistic competition in the world market. This introduced the centrifugal forces that ultimately led to the break-up of the common market and, in so doing, consolidated the international concentration and centralization of capital under the iron heel of international finance capital.

Developing A Monetary Economy

In Uganda the policies outlined in the First Five Year Development Plan[1] (Plan I), derived from the policy position of the World Bank, were primarily agricultural and aimed at increasing cotton production, while reducing that of coffee because of unfavourable world prices. To achieve these targets, support was given to the 'progressive farmer' and where this was not possible, particularly in cotton production, the group farm was used to raise production levels.

The Plan pointed out that, in order to achieve these goals it was also necessary to provide credit facilities or subsidies in kind to the peasantry. A number of credit schemes started during the colonial period were continued and new ones created. The finance for these schemes came mainly from the peasants themselves, in so far as the funds were drawn from the government's coffee and cotton price assistance funds. These were managed by the Uganda Credit and Savings Bank and later by the Uganda Commercial Bank.

The Second Five Year Development Plan[2] (Plan II) essentially continued and refined the policy of reducing the 'overproduction' of coffee while also seeking to supplement coffee and cotton as the 'main spearhead of development' by creating a more diversified agriculture. The strategy once again involved giving credit to the peasants to engage in other crops, while at the same time maintaining the production levels of cotton and coffee.

In order to induce a monetary economy separate from the subsistence economy, the peasants were encouraged 'to grow at least one cash crop'. An Agricultural Produce Marketing Board (A.P.M.B.) was set up with the advice and technical assistance of GATT, to help the peasants 'to enter fully into the cash economy' by producing tea, sugar, groundnuts, cocoa, rubber, etc. More group farms were created, adding another 100 to the existing 40. Three types of credit scheme to provide short-, medium- and long-term loans were set up to achieve this. The co-operative movement was increasingly used in mobilizing resources.

The credits provided in both the first and second periods were in many cases never repaid. Due to the high level of default during Plan I, some of the group farms were closed. Moreover, since the wages paid to the peasants on these group farms were very low, the peasants invariably gave first priority to their own farms to produce subsistence crops.

Despite these problems in the rural credit system, overall performance for the two crops in the first period was considered satisfactory. Cotton production rose from 371,000 bales in 1961 to 460,000 bales in 1969–70, partly due to the use of insecticides, fertilizers and other techniques, but particularly because of the introduction of new varieties of the high-yield cotton seed, SATU and B.P.A. Nevertheless, Plan II's target of 550,000 bales failed to materialize. Coffee production fell slightly in 1967–8 but then picked up again so that, by 1971, there was an 'overproduction'.

The A.P.M.B. was in the meantime having difficulty collecting and selling the small crops. Yet the drive to turn the peasantry wholly into cash crop producers meant that the small subsistence crops were now sold, collected and marketed by the A.P.M.B. and so caught up in the inflationary pressures that were emerging in the economy as a whole in 1969–70.

The growth in agricultural output was never reflected in the wages of the peasantry. While the wages for coffee and cotton in 1958 (itself a depression period) stood at 80 cts. and 58 cts. a pound respectively, they fell over the years until they reached the low level of 50 cts. and 40 cts., at a time when prices of manufactures in the highly protected import-substitution industries were rising steadily. In the agricultural sector, therefore, this period saw the imperialist monopolies reap the benefits of cheaply produced commodities while the peasantry financed their own exploitation by providing the credit and disposing of 'their' commodities at the lowest prices on the world market.

In industry, as we have noted in the first section of this chapter, tariff protection and other incentives were offered to monopolies to pursue import-substitution in Uganda. The two Plans emphasized this as well. Plan I, which prioritized agriculture, at the same time reiterated its intention to develop manufacturing as a way of counteracting 'the vagaries of the overseas markets and primary products'. The Plan listed a number of ventures in which it considered the monopolies might find it profitable to invest in joint ownership with the Uganda Development Corporation (U.D.C.). It projected a modest

Shs. 140 million investment in the Plan period, concentrating on the agricultural processing and semi-processing sector, with some import substitution, particularly in industries 'naturally protected' by transport costs, such as beer, furniture, building materials and suitcases, as well as those producing perishables and services and public utilities.

Plan II was more adventurous in emphasizing the need to turn Uganda's economy into a 'predominantly industrial economy' in the long run. It was now argued that the lack of a 'sizeable industrial sector' worsened Uganda's precarious position in the world market; industrialization would provide the 'primary basis' for growth and stability. The growth of import substitution industries had implications for the existing common market arrangement in East Africa, and Uganda glimpsed the possibility of additional markets in the Sudan, the Congo, Rwanda and Burundi. Import substitution was also seen as a basis for creating employment and 'saving' foreign exchange, as well as reducing imports.[3] An investment of Shs. 900 million over the Plan period was envisaged, with an annual growth rate of 10%.

The Plan I industrial projections were mainly achieved. International monopoly capital seized the opportunity and a number of new industries were opened in this early period. British finance capital took 80% of the East African market in hoe manufacturing; and also invested in a distillery, chemicals, etc; Italian monopoly capital joined with local capital from the Madhvan group in steel production; while Japanese monopolies were quick to jostle with the British in the textile sector, specializing in garments, in a joint venture with the U.D.C. and local investors. As a result the projected investment target was exceeded.

Plan II also attracted new investment, but despite the optimism of the plan, the end results began to reveal the weaknesses in the strategy. Forty per cent of the new investment in the initial period went into expanding the existing sugar, beer, shoe, blanket, oil milling, printing and soap industries. New investment took place in food canning, textiles, clothing, metals, paper bags, plastics, ceramics, glass and batteries. Encouraging as this was, the government was concerned that very little of this industrialization was linking up together. For instance, apart from building materials, virtually no intermediate goods were being produced.

Returning to a problem already evident in Plan I, it was noted that industry in Uganda was 'still highly dependent on imported raw materials and that virtually no industries buy any of their intermediate goods from other manufacturing establishments in Uganda'.[4] Imports had also increased and little new employment was being created. The imported materials therefore formed a 'particularly high percentage' of the value of the final product.

The reality of neo-colonialism was beginning to tell. The neo-colonial regime could not understand the mechanisms of transnational corporate strategy. Protected and induced, it imported inputs duty-free on the basis of their cheapness. Rather than planning for an integrated economy, its objective was, on the contrary, to integrate production and markets in Uganda with production and markets on a world scale. In other words, the arrangement was exactly suitable for integrating the Ugandan economy with the transnational monopolies of the various imperialist countries, whether Uganda was in the East African common market or not. And this is what was also happening elsewhere in East Africa.

Transnational Integration

By 1966-67 the performance in the import-substitution sector had begun to slow down, due partly to the declining export market prospects in Kenya and Tanzania. But still the monopolies were prepared to invest in new lines — cardboard boxes, transistor radios, batteries, plastic sheeting, floor tiles and bottles, and a bakery and new cement factory at Kasese were built. New plants in ceramics and tyre retreading were also projected, and in 1969 it was planned to bring in new joint ventures for knitwear, glass, brakelinings, a second asbestos plant and a paper industry, with an electric bulb factory to be added in 1970.

All these developments complicated the import substitution network in East Africa and the market in the region, but so long as investors were protected within the Ugandan market this did not matter, for the same monopolies who partnered with the U.D.C. and local Ugandan capitalists were also operating in the other two equally protected markets, catering mainly for high income consumers.

The target growth rate of 7.2% over the entire plan period did not materialize in 1971, reaching only 5.8%. Despite the much-heralded optimism about industrialization being the 'primary basis' for growth, all this manufacturing activity, as a percentage of total output, increased by a bare 0.4% and accounted for 12% of G.D.P. as compared to 12% at the beginning of the Plan II period, the highest rate of growth being in food manufacturing and small industry. Employment in manufacturing increased by only 6.2%, very much below target. It even fell in the textile industry, despite the new plant in Mbale. As Baryaruha noted,[5] tariff protection attracted capital-intensive techniques; the increase in employment was only in absolute terms and, when population increase is taken into account, it had in fact declined overall. Plan III, published under the new military regime, blamed this on the slow growth in manufacturing output.

The position of workers in industry was increasingly encroached upon by capital at the insistence of the monopolies and the neo-colonial state. As in Kenya and Tanzania, after the Turner Report on wages, it was decided that wage 'restraint' would attract investment. As a result, Plan II stipulated that wage increases must be held at 1% overall per annum, with those earning as little as £90 a year getting a maximum of 3.5%, and those earning £600 a year and over getting no increase at all. One of the obscure rationalizations for this, in line with similar themes in Tanzania, was that further increases would create a wider gap with rural incomes, since all the workers would not be 'benefiting equally from the development effort'. This wage restraint, the government noted, resulted in a rapid growth in investment.[6] Finally, labour legislation restricted the workers' right to strike, with President Obote declaring that under Independence the right to strike was 'archaic' in principle and in practice.

Uganda's transnational corporate integration was also manifested in this period by her multilateralized trade links, reflecting the loss of hegemony of British bilateral imperialism in Uganda. Whereas, in the period up to 1945, all Uganda's export and import links were with the U.K. and the Sterling Area, particularly India, by the 1950s they began to diversify. By 1969, apart from the intra-East African trade, the U.S. had taken over as Uganda's main customer, mostly of coffee; with the U.K. following in second place and Japan in the third. The U.K. maintained her lead as exporter of capital goods to Uganda, but Japan began to increase her share in the following years. Consistent with her investment, Japan exported to Uganda synthetic and artificial fabrics as well as motor vehicles. The multilateral integration of Uganda was further strengthened by an agreement (later consolidated in the Lome Convention) with the European Economic Community to establish a free trade area with the three East African nations.

Uganda's new position was further reflected in its sources of finance. We have already noted that Plan I relied on 73% external financing, though only 59% was actually forthcoming and local financing had to be produced from taxes. Plan II was less reliant on external financing, having taken measures to mobilize local funds through such measures as restructuring the banking and financial system. These local resources were, however, themselves increasingly tied to foreign finance capital and fully utilized by the monopolies for their purposes. By 1970 the neo-colonial regime openly acknowledged the fact that the U.K. was no longer the dominant source of Uganda's 'development' finance: 'Moreover U.K. is no longer the largest single donor, either in terms of gross loans or annual disbursements.' In a mood of obedience to international finance, it explained, 'In addition, there has been considerable diversification of aid sources and this has been handled without loss of efficiency.'[8] These new sources of finance consisted of 25 different countries and international organizations. The Plan noted that the I.D.A. (an associate of the World Bank) had recently announced the tripling of aid to Uganda and had become the major financier of projects connected with education, agriculture and transport. During the Plan II period Uganda had been offered official 'aid' of Shs. 976 million, of which Shs. 679.9 million had been utilized.

The nationalization measures of 1969 were mainly in response to the disappointing performance of Plan II, and were inspired by the possibility that a 'Move to the Left' strategy would give the state better powers to mobilize resources and direct the economy. Most of these schemes had been only partially implemented when the coup d'état took place in early 1971.

The Third Five Year Development Plan (Plan III)[9] reversed these measures and accused the civilian regime of acting harshly towards international finance capital. It proposed a modification of the terms of the takeovers in order to attract more foreign capital. The military regime's gestures to the British imperialists, in particular, were supposed to be a homage to their role in the ousting of the civilian regime. Britain did make use of this to reassert her position politically, but imperialist rivalries soon created new imbalances in the situation. Measures to boost agricultural production and industry were soon overshadowed by new 'revolutionary' measures of the 'economic war' and the subsequent takeover of Indian, Israeli and British interests in Uganda.

The short-lived honeymoon with Britain and Israel did not halt the imperialist integration of Uganda's economy to its needs. The ensuing 'economic war' was a severe blow to agricultural production and industry, creating a very high level of inflation in the economy, and thereby pushing many peasants back into subsistence cultivation. This dislocation in the neo-colonial economy naturally impelled the regime to act and attract new capital in transport and communications, agriculture and industry.

The 'Action Programme' (Plan IV),[10] announced at the end of 1977, was accompanied by a further decree for the protection of new investment, giving even more benefits to international interests in return for a projected 80% contribution of foreign capital towards the budget of Shs. 11,000 million. German, Italian and British monopolies began to seize this new opportunity, but due to the continuing crisis of the Ugandan neo-colonial formation and the insecurity caused by the military dictatorship, such efforts to inject large doses of private investment were unsuccessful. Nevertheless, Uganda continued to be tied to the production needs of the monopolies, and the disintegration of the East African common market was not shaken by the integration of the Ugandan economy into the world market.

The exploitation and domination of Uganda is apparent in the vast incomes and super-profits siphoned out of the country by the monopolies. While figures show that, between 1966 and 1971, there was a total inflow of both short-term and long-term capital of Shs. 139.24 million, the outflows on the same account were Shs. 335.40 million, thus giving a net negative balance of Shs. 196.16 million overall.

The inter-state flow of funds within East Africa, reflecting the interests of international finance capital in microcosm, revealed the same pattern. Between 1966 and 1971 there was a net outflow of funds from Uganda, mainly to Kenya, the net outflow to Kenya offsetting the net inflow from Tanzania. The total inflows were Shs. 232.52 million in 1968, Shs. 226.69 million in 1969, Shs. 296.41 million in 1970 and Shs. 283.51 million in 1971. The total outflows to the other two partner states were Shs. 452.96 million in 1968, Shs. 532.06 million in 1969, Shs. 522.21 million in 1970 and Shs. 566.79 million in 1971. The outflows to the East African Corporations (for repatriation to the Crown Agents for loan repayments) accounted for about 20% of the gross outflows over this period. The outflows to Kenya were merely a convenient channel to the outside world, since Kenya was itself in net deficit, particularly after 1970, as we shall see in the next chapter. Overall, therefore, the neo-colonial economy in Uganda was merely an appendage to the wider exploitative arrangements imposed on the country by multilateral imperialism. Under the cover of regional co-operation with neighbouring countries, the horizontal linkage was but a conduit through which vast sums were siphoned off to the metropolitan regions of the world, leaving behind a crisis within the neo-colonial political economy reflected in the political instability of the region as a whole and of Uganda in particular.[11]

References

1. Uganda Government, *The First Five Year Development Plan 1961/62-1965/66* (Entebbe, Government Printer, 1961).
2. Uganda Government, *Work for Progress: Uganda's Second Five Year Plan 1966-1971* (Entebbe, Government Printer, 1966).
3. W.W. Kalema, 'Private Enterprise in Uganda' in P.A. Thomas, *Private Enterprise and the East African Company* (Dar es Salaam, Tanzania Publishing House, 1969).
4. Uganda Government, *Background to the Budget 1967-68* (Entebbe, Government Printer).
5. A. Baryaruha, *Factors Affecting Industrial Employment: A Study of Ugandan Experience, 1954-1964* (London, Oxford University Press, 1967).
6. Uganda Government, *Background to the Budget 1968-69* (Entebbe, Government Printer).
7. Uganda Government, *Background to the Budget, 1970-71* (Entebbe, Government Printer, 1972), p. 78.
8. *Ibid.*, p. 79.
9. Uganda Government, *The Third Five Year Development Plan* (Entebbe, Government Printer, 1977).
10. Uganda Government, *Action Programme.*
11. For further details, see D.W. Nabudere, *Imperialism and Revolution in Uganda* (London/Dar es Salaam, Onyx/Tanzania Publishing House, 1980).

9. The Kenyan Neo-Colonial Economy

Whereas the World Bank missions to East Africa had argued for an increasingly active economic role for the state in the case of Tanzania, and a kind of mixed private capital/parastatal role for Uganda, in the case of Kenya the neo-colonial regime was warned to 'keep hands off' as far as private enterprise was concerned, and this determined all the recommendations for Kenya's strategy in neo-colonial integration with transnational capital.

Kenya's Development Programme 1960/3 (First Plan) had already emphasized the role of private foreign investment in the country's development effort.[1] According to the then self-proclaimed spokesman of U.S. finance capital, Tom Mboya, 'private enterprise supplies incentives for domestic saving and innovation, and induces the inflow of foreign capital, knowledge and skills which could not otherwise be obtained.'

> Our firm encouragement of private enterprise in Kenya is not evidence of a blind dedication to a form of ownership and management, but rather to a conviction that this form of enterprise, in suitable conjunction with other forms, can assist us in promoting the welfare of our citizens. This is the standard that must always be satisfied.[2]

Thus the role of the neo-colonial state was to provide adequate incentives to the investors by identifying opportunities for private investment, stimulating the application (and combination) of foreign and local capital, and enforcing an incomes policy. Mboya added:

> Planning for private sector development in Kenya takes the form of identifying and assigning priorities to investment and production opportunities, and assisting those of greatest importance through the provision of capital, advice and protection.[3]

In a broad policy document which his Ministry supervised[4] the government spelt out a strategy on these lines and played down any need for nationalization. Noting the interests of those who had taken the first opportunity to line their pockets with the 'fruits of Uhuru', it warned: 'If the policy [i.e. nationalization] were applied to an economic activity, such as bus transportation, it would affect everyone, African and otherwise, owning productive resources in the industry.'[5]

No wonder, then, that the First Plan was optimistic about the inflow of foreign capital: 90% of the capital required for implementing the Plan was expected to come from external sources. This very high figure *excluded* the official aid for the land settlement programme suggested by the World Bank and the British Government.

Private Capital and Agriculture

Of the projected finances under the First Plan, 35% was earmarked for agriculture, with another 3.4% from the settlement programme monies. Among other things this money went into land adjudication and registration, in conformity with the Swynnerton Plan, and into schemes to encourage Africans to produce cash crops. Even though the major push in the agricultural sector was connected with land settlements, by 1963 less than 4,000 European settlers still owned some 6.5 million acres of the best land in the country, forming four-fifths of the total area with reasonable and reliable rainfall. The transfer of land and the orderly settlement of Africans in some of these areas was carried out in order to 'restore the confidence' of white farmers who had been in a panic about their future.

The consolidation of private property in land, as part of the policy of mollifying land hunger, together with the need to build up a credit system for small farmers, provided a policy suited to the British view of future developments in Kenya. Unlike Uganda and Tanganyika, Kenya had a severe shortage of good land. In order to maintain the production system to the advantage of international finance capital, private property in land and large-scale farming had to be preserved as far as possible.

The first settlement scheme was implemented in 1961 (and modified a year later) with a loan of Shs. 150 million from Britain and the World Bank. As a result, a number of African 'yeoman' farmers and small-holding peasants were granted titles to land, but this settlement was limited to the fringes of the former Highlands adjacent to the reserves.[6] The later expansion in the 'Million Acre Scheme', together with the Harambee Scheme announced by President Kenyatta, resulted altogether in a 1½ million acres of settlement schemes.

This early push for settling small farmers was concerned to satisfy the immediate problem of land hunger that had been behind the national movement, and once the Million Acre Scheme had been completed steps were taken to halt any further settlements of this kind. In the Second Plan period, although 16% of the budget was to be used for further settlement, a change in policy reoriented the whole exercise towards the expansion of large farms. A British mission in 1965 recommended that, in order to 'avoid any possible catastrophe', the Kenya Government should 'reassess' the economics of the settlements. Led by Maxwell Stamp, the mission included Swynnerton

himself, the former colonial expert who had advised on the land consolidation policy in the 1950s. The Stamp Mission pointed out that the
Kenyan Government's projected loan from Britain of Shs. 700 million to settle
farmers over the next 15 years would 'saddle' Kenya with a heavy debt
burden for 'little economic advantage'. Instead, the mission recommended
free market transactions in land, and concluded:

> The Mission is agreed that, were it not for the political pressures, it
> would be better not to have a further programme which involves the
> deliberate transfer, with government assistance and subsidy, of
> European farms to African hands. If political pressures make a pro-
> gramme necessary, the smaller and slower the buy-out programme . . .
> the better for Kenya — and the British tax-payer.[7]

Thus the crucial objective of the national movement was to be evaded.
The Second Plan,[8] for the period 1966–70, declared that no funds would be
provided for land settlement as it had been 'largely attained'. The 'Two
million Acre Scheme' announced by Kenyatta in 1964 was abandoned.
Settlement was now represented as 'expensive' and as 'conferring privileges
on a few at the expense of the many'.[9] The Plan argued that the debt burden
of Shs. 320 million which would have been incurred by 1968 to finance the
existing farms would be too heavy a load 'on the rest of the economy and
hold up the development of other sectors'.[10]

Although fresh political pressure for land in 1970 resulted in another
free grant of Shs. 50 million from the British Government, the 150,000
acres were not made available to the peasants. In the meantime, over 1.6
million acres were being sold in straightforward commercial transactions to
large farmers, financed by the Agricultural Finance Corporation and the
Agricultural Development Corporation and excluding the small farmers.
Altogether, by 1970 Shs. 400 million had been spent recovering farms from
white settlers and transferring them to the African farmers.

To suit the new conditions of neo-colonialism, about half of these lands
went to large African farmers, who equally depended on credit to maintain
production. Many former white settlers acted as managers of these large
farms now owned by capitalist African farmers. The interests between the
two somehow coincided; as the Stamp Mission had stated in 1965, these
African large-scale farmers tended 'to identify themselves economically with
the large-scale European farmers' who still remained in some areas.[11] The
African large-scale farmers also felt that there should only be a 'slow transfer
of farms' because of the need 'to retain European expertise'. The mission was
'impressed by the broad view taken by these farmers', concerned not only
with their own interest, but with the 'national need to increase food production, employment and agricultural exports'.[12]

While this concurrence of class interest was taking root, the position of
the landless was getting more precarious. The poor and medium producer,
burdened with indebtedness as a result of exploitation (which burden was

being reinforced by the new credit institutions and the legal requirements to register and obtain a land title) were forced to sell up, thus helping the larger farmers to concentrate their holdings even more.

This was how the World Bank's dictum that private investment in land should be maintained was put into effect. Production grew at about 4.5% per annum, which was seen as a great success for the strategy. The Third Plan[13] pointed specifically to the need to 'complete the Kenyanization of large-scale mixed farms and to make substantial progress towards Kenyanization of ranches and plantations'.[14] While noting that 'evidence available' suggested that most farm products could be produced 'very successfully' on small-scale farms with the implication that 'in the long run' a considerable amount of land currently used for large-scale farming would have to be subdivided, its basic sympathies were still with the large-scale farmer. It pointed out that, in 1972, the large farmers produced 48% of gross marketed agricultural production and were 'significant employers of labour'. It followed that large-scale farming would be kept 'intact' to the extent necessary to ensure sufficient supplies of those products that could be produced on a large-scale basis.[15]

The bias in favour of the big farmer was also reflected at the level of credit. Of the total loan portfolio of Shs. 284 million, in 1972 Shs. 240 million was lent to 2,500 large farmers and ranchers, while only Shs. 50 million went to 14,500 small-scale farmers.[16] The Third Plan provided for a further Shs. 100 million to be lent to the large farmers. In this way the confidence of European farmers was 'restored' as the economy continued on a course to secure the interests of the imperialist states, for whom the production was being carried out and who provided some of the finances for this expansion.

Manufacturing and Industrialization

In manufacturing the neo-colonial regime also went out of its way to attract private capital. In the words of the Second Plan: 'It is the Government policy to offer inducements, equally available to both new and existing firms, to encourage private industry to play its full role in the development of Kenya.'[17] It pointed to the combination of incentives and incomes policy as tools for inducing private capital investment, and repeated that in special cases the government might initiate feasibility studies designed to attract [private] investment. The Third Plan laid down the main policies for attaining a level of industrialization, which were the very policies most desired by the transnational corporations: Kenyans were encouraged to 'manage' industry and participate as investors. A continued restriction of imports, implying a policy of import substitution on the basis of tariff protection, was stipulated. The increase in the degree of 'government participation' was limited to promoting and financing some new projects. The 'degree of processing of raw materials', currently being exported, was to be increased as a major component in the 'employment-intensive industrialization' strategy.

This policy of import substitution encouraged a high level of investment by transnational monopolies. While locally owned companies engaged in the processing of cereals (maize and wheat), foreign investment moved into other sectors of food and agricultural processing, and into certain areas of industrial activity, in particular tea, coffee and sisal. Meat and fruit canning also attracted both British and U.S. monopolies, with Brook Bond-Liebig and Del Monte as the front runners. To this was added the earlier import substitution in textiles, footwear, made-up clothing, assembly industries and paper products.

The foreign capital component can be judged from the fact that in 1966 long-term capital inflows amounted to 35% of expenditure in manufacturing, and 42% in 1968 — a high level of foreign enterprise in manufacturing and one that enabled the monopolies to tie down a lot of local capital.[18] The paper by Herman,[19] used by the I.L.O. in its Report, gives a picture of the degree of foreign enterprise control over local resources. It shows that in 1967 and 1968 local capital tied up in enterprises involving foreign capital constituted only 12.5% and 15% of the total capital invested in these enterprises. Taking other figures into account, the I.L.O. Report reckons that foreign enterprise accounted for 57% and 60% of the total manufacturing investment in these two years, 1966 and 1968. Of course, this is a very crude way of understanding the problem, since the foreign monopolies also had access to local resources not included in these calculations, for example, low water and electricity charges, and local services such as free or cheap access roads and sidings, as well as lower tax rates, tariff protection, and remissions of duties, etc.

But the calculation does give an idea of the process of concentration and centralization of local capital under the compulsion of international finance capital operating in Kenya — which is, of course, why the monopolies invested in the country. While the neo-colonial regime thought it could manage foreign capital as part of a judicious 'development programme', the transnational corporations were perfectly aware of the opportunity for mobilizing and applying these local resources to its own production needs.

This 'inducement' to foreign capital 'succeeded' in that it attracted a very high level of capital import. For the three years 1967 to 1970 the average annual rate of inflow was Shs. 206 million, resulting in a total inflow since independence of Shs. 826 million, which went mainly to manufacturing.[20] Most of this, it should be noted, was a ploughing back of profits. This investment was attracted by the high level of profitability that the policy of highly protected import substitution implied.

These monopolies, which in 1967 accounted for 57% of total output and an even higher percentage (65%) in 1972, reaped, according to the I.L.O. Report, 'a disproportionally large share of profits' of 73% of the entire manufacturing sector.[21] These were the firms, the Report noted, with local equity participation. It also states that these high profits were in industries where the foreign monopolies had no competition, in other words, in industries where they enjoyed 'temporary local monopoly', reinforced by the protection granted them by the neo-colonial state.

Working on the basis of the paper by Phelps and Wasow, which demonstrated that effective protection was relatively high in some of the sectors in which foreign enterprise was dominant, the I.L.O. concluded that foreign enterprise controlled 'a very large part of the gross product and, more important, an even larger part of the surplus in the manufacturing sector'.[22] Phelps and Wasow further revealed that effective protection was as high as 172.9% in sugar and 82.9% in rope, cord and twine. Of the 37 firms they examined 16 ranked in the 'first three digit groups' in terms of effective protection.[23]

In terms of distribution of industry, the I.L.O. Report noted that foreign capital was greatest in petroleum refining, tobacco, cement, metal products (mainly cans) and textiles. It was also predominant in consumer goods and 'where brand names and product differentiation are important sources of competitive advantage', i.e. tobacco, textiles and miscellaneous foods (particularly baby foods and prepared cereals), footwear and clothing, paint, soap and miscellaneous chemicals (printing inks, household polishes, cosmetics, toiletries, miscellaneous drugs and tonics) and pharmaceutical products (including patent medicines). In these areas, the Report noted, gross production by foreign firms accounted for more than 75% of the total and for 30% of all gross production by foreign-owned firms.[24]

Vertical Integration vs. Federation

The I.L.O.'s observations are important in enabling us to comprehend the forces at work in the political economy of Kenya, particularly how they related to the new forces of integration that tended to militate against national or regional integration and political federation. They reveal that Kenya, just like the other two territories, was being integrated vertically with transnational monopolies through the bargaining strength of the monopolies themselves and the eagerly conceded protection offered by the neo-colonial states. Thus the monopolies were able to achieve their aim, namely to make profits — *super-profits*.

Despite the illusions of the petty bourgeoisie in these territories, who saw this process as a basis for national development and growth in creating employment, reducing imports and, therefore, 'saving foreign exchange', the might of the international capitalist monopolies made such hopes unrealizable from the outset. The I.L.O. Report noted, for one thing, that the import-substitution industries tended to be capital intensive and were only more labour intensive than local ones where both foreign and locally owned enterprises participated in the same industry. This was because foreign enterprises had more skilled supervisers, which enabled them to use production techniques based on low-cost unskilled labour; local enterprises without skilled supervisory labour tended to take on expensive capital-saving techniques to save on supervision. This applied in grain milling, baking, clothing and made-up clothing, beer and malt, furniture, paper and paper products, non-electric machinery and miscellaneous manufactures.[25] Thus employment prospects were minimal, as was evident in the failure to reach targets of 15% and 10% employment increases agreed between the workers, the monopolies and the state under the first and second Tripartite Agreements of 1964 and 1970. Under the second Agreement employment rose by only 7.3% between 1970 and 1971, while the monopolies happily reaped the higher profits resulting from the agreed wage freezes.

The claim that foreign capital tended to supplement local resources is equally shown to be a myth. It is more correct to say, as we have seen and as Tom Mboya correctly pointed out, that foreign capital does not contribute to the 'domestic ownership of assets',[26] but rather that it 'taps domestic capital' – and not in order to train Kenyans, as Mboya imagined, but in order to make super-profits. Such training is of no consequence if, rather than leading to the development of national resources, it siphons them off for the transnational monopolies.

To be sure, such tapping of local resources was made possible by the neo-colonial state itself through such institutions as the Industrial and Commercial Development Corporation (I.C.D.C.) and other finance houses and commercial banks. The later restriction on local borrowing facilities by transnational capital to 20% of their foreign equity contribution did not change the position significantly since it failed to restrict borrowing from public institutions like the I.C.D.C. itself, whose loans had in some years been greater than the equity brought in by the monopolies, as noted by the I.L.O. Report.[27]

Moreover, foreign enterprises were allowed to issue shares on the local stock exchange with the approval of the Capital Issues Committee of the Treasury. It was on this basis, according to the Report, that for the period 1964–70 about 30% of all local private and public capital invested in manufacturing went to foreign-owned companies. This, of course, ignores the fact that most of the capital presented in the statistics as 'foreign investment' was in fact locally derived profit which had simply been reinvested.

Foreign Capital and Imports

As has been shown of Uganda, it is not correct to link the attraction of foreign capital with a reduction of imports. In Kenya imports actually tended to increase as import substitution progressed. By 1971 imports were 62% higher than in 1969. This can be partly attributed to the effects of the incentives granted to the monopolies to import machinery duty free and the right to reimbursement of duty on imported raw materials. It is for this reason that, as has been noted for Uganda and Tanganyika, the linkages both forward and backward tended to be very weak.

To compound the problem further, there was no way of saving foreign exchange when importation from the monopolies increased and, particularly, when the surplus value created in the country was siphoned off by various means. The I.L.O. Report noted that Kenya had been 'very easy-going' in permitting the subsidiaries of foreign firms to make payments freely to the

parent company in respect of research and development services, other
technical services, management fees, etc. 'in addition' to royalties and the
transfer of dividends and profits. It added: 'This can result in a considerable
[outward] flow of funds – far in excess of declared profits.'[28] While aware
of Kenya's 20% 'withholding tax' on technical payments, it nevertheless
warned that many techniques of siphoning funds out of the country were
being used, including the transfer pricing of imports and exports and transfer
accounting techniques which enabled the monopolies to maximize profits
(by minimizing their tax commitments) 'over the whole of their international
operations' by moving resources from one country to another.

The transfer pricing technique was particularly used in import-substitution
industries in a well-protected market, such as the three East African countries.
The monopolies could reduce their 'value-added', and hence local taxes on
profits, by over-invoicing imports or under-invoicing exports. While the I.L.O.
Report found little evidence of under-invoicing in Kenya, it nevertheless
noted 'some evidence of over-invoicing'[29] at 20 to 30% by certain monopolies on intermediate goods, i.e. spares and accessories imported from the
parent companies. The Report suspected that this technique was resorted to
by monopolies which had shown consistent losses over periods of four and
five years, this representing a sizeable loss of tax revenue for the country.

Colin Leys also observes that, if over-invoicing outside the import-substitution sector was taken into account, and adjustment made on the official
statistics of private capital repatriation, we would get a figure of the order of
£1,600 million over the years 1964–70.[30] This means that there was a vast
outflow (probably twice as big as the private capital inflow), if we note that
in the period 1967–70 the officially recorded private capital inflow was
Shs. .519 million, of which on average 56% was retained profits, against an
outflow of Shs. .443 million.[31] Thus the neo-colonial state neither created
employment for the people consistent with population growth, nor 'saved
foreign exchange' for any other purpose, but merely acted as the mechanism
for exploiting the working people and draining Kenya of her resources for
the benefit of transnational monopolies which the neo-colonial state served
under a new form of vertical integration with these monopolies. In the second
volume of this work we shall argue that, contrary to the arguments of Uganda
and Tanzania, Kenya was 'gaining' nothing out of the East African arrangement, by way of actual development.

A 'Turning Point'

The pattern of rapid growth in the Kenyan economy that emerged on the
basis of this externally oriented economy catering for monopoly interests
was bound to come to grief. All the flowery trappings merely concealed the
fact that the benefits of the economy were going to the international
monopolies and the minute minority of local compradorial elements. The
siphoning off of the country's resources at the rate indicated above was the
return for the easy growth rates of the first six years of Independence. By
1970 this vast outflow began to be felt as a balance of payments problem,

and this affected the relations between the three East African countries co-operating within the East African Community.

The 1972 I.L.O. findings were in marked contrast to the 1960s, 'when Kenya seemed to have solved the problem of reconciling economic growth with a strong balance of payments'.[32] In that period receipts for transport, tourism and other services accruing to Kenya's central position in the economy of the region as a whole had bolstered the economy for the monopolies. Capital had 'poured in' while foreign exchange reserves 'mounted'. The first signs that the situation was 'precarious' had appeared in 1970, 'when imports rose sharply', as they did again in 1971, reaching a level of 50% above that of 1969.

The rise in export figures, due to the 1970 rise in coffee prices, was thus offset by the rise in imports the following year. The I.L.O. Report observed: 'Meanwhile the rise in exports petered out and the inflows of capital decreased. Foreign exchange reserves sank . . . .' And while the government took immediate measures to prevent the drain of foreign exchange reserves by imposing limits on commercial credit and higher taxes, measures which might well have reversed the rise in imports without causing acute scarcities, the point still remained that 'the myth of effortless growth, a Kenyan "miracle", had been shattered'.[33] It appeared to the I.L.O. therefore, that the inflow of private and official capital was having the adverse effect 'which had generally been welcome as a means of increasing investment and stimulating growth'. These inflows were now felt to be 'insufficient to fill the gap'.[34]

The change was also noticed by the World Bank in a new study of the Kenyan economy,[35] which pointed out that, while Kenya had achieved an unequalled rate of economic growth of 7% per year between 1964 and 1972, there were 'two facets' of her past performance which were 'less satisfactory' and which should have received 'careful attention' in devising a strategy for the second decade. The first was the Government's failure to distribute the benefits of development as widely as would have been expected to counteract the 'twin problems' of unemployment and 'continuing poverty'. The second 'worrying aspect', which was 'harder to define' (*sic*), was a variety of factors which 'had started to emerge' in the economy and which would cause recurring problems unless they were removed soon. These were the temptations either to resort to inflationary 'financing tactics' or 'desperate measures to combat unemployment which we are sure Kenya can and will avoid'. It added further: 'For example, it appears that the policy of protecting import substitution industries may, in fact, increase Kenya's dependence on imports, and conflict with the goal of promoting agriculture and rural development.'[36]

The Bank then concluded that Kenya's performance since Independence had not been 'quite as good as first appears'. Kenya 'had reached a turning point in development where she is at the end of the first "easy" stage of growth and is facing growing resource constraints, as is indicated by the tighter fiscal position, balance of payments pressure, and the first serious impact of inflation'. In the second decade the government would have to raise more local resources and embark on a new line of recommended policies to attract a lower inflow of foreign capital.

Yet it should be remembered that the policies that led to this 'turning point' were the very ones recommended by the World Bank itself and dutifully implemented by the Kenyan Government; what was happening was that the Bank, having achieved its first objective for the monopolies, was now devising a new strategy for them for the next decade (which unfortunately we cannot go into in this work). The first objective, achieved in a clearer manner in Kenya but no less elsewhere — had been, as Morgan's survey revealed, to allow the investing monopolies to reap a sufficient return in four years to repatriate the original investment. This having been achieved, the monopolies needed new assurances against practices which tended to 'frighten' investors, namely some aspects of trade policy, Kenyanization, import restrictions and other inflationary tactics. The same fears were being voiced in Tanzania and Uganda and represented a new stage in the consolidation of neo-colonialism.

References

1. Kenya Government, *The Development Programme 1960-63* (Nairobi, Government Printer, 1960).
2. T. Mboya, 'The Role of the Private Sector in Kenyan National Development' in P.A. Thomas, *Private Enterprise and the East African Company* (Dar es Salaam, Tanzania Publishing House, 1967), p. 195.
3. *Ibid.,* p. 196.
4. Kenya Government, *African Socialism and its Application to Planning in Kenya* (Nairobi, Government Printer, 1965).
5. Kenya Government, *African Socialism.*
6. Colin Leys, *Underdevelopment in Kenya: The Political Economy of Neo-Colonialism, 1964-70* (London, Heinemann, 1975).
7. Stamp Report quoted in Leys, *op. cit.,* p. 88.
8. Kenya Government, *Development Plan 1966-70* (Nairobi, Government Printer, 1966).
9. Leys, *op. cit.,* p. 83.
10. Kenya Government, *Development Plan, op. cit.,* p. 15.
11. Stamp Report, in Leys, *op. cit.,* p. 38.
12. *Ibid.*
13. Kenya Government, *Development Plan, 1974-78,* Part I (Nairobi, Government Printer, 1974).
14. *Ibid.,* p. 197.
15. *Ibid.,* p. 199.
16. *Ibid.,* pp. 212–13.
17. *Ibid.,* p. 39.
18. International Labour Organization, *Employment, Incomes and Equality in Kenya* (Geneva, I.L.O., 1972).

19. B. Herman, 'Some Basic Data for Analysing the Political Economy of Foreign Investment in Kenya', I.D.S. Discussion Paper No. 112 (University of Nairobi, 1971).
20. *Ibid.*,
21. I.L.O., *op. cit.*, pp. 184, 442.
22. *Ibid.*, p. 446.
23. Phelps and Wasow, 'Measuring Protection and its Effects on Kenya', I.D.S. Discussion Paper (University of Nairobi, 1970).
24. I.L.O., *op. cit.*
25. *Ibid.*, p. 450; see also D.W. Nabudere, *The Political Economy of Imperialism* (London/Dar es Salaam, Zed Press/Tanzania Publishing House, 1977), pp. 53–4.
26. Mboya, *op. cit.*, p. 201.
27. I.L.O., *op. cit.*, p. 452.
28. *Ibid.*, pp. 455–6.
29. *Ibid.*, pp. 136, 453–7, 463.
30. C. Leys, *op. cit.*, pp. 137–8.
31. See I.L.O., *op. cit.*, Table 37, p. 136.
32. *Ibid.*, p. 98.
33. *Ibid.*, pp. 98–9.
34. I.L.O., *Report.*
35. I.B.R.D., *Kenya: Into the Second Decade* (Baltimore, Johns Hopkins, 1975).
36. *Ibid.*, pp. 5–6.

10. Continue the Struggle for National Independence

The recognition of the right of the peoples of East Africa to self-determination was an important and significant political victory, securing territorial separation from the British Empire and recognition of their equality in the sphere of international politics and law with other states. The major point that emerges, however, is that the attainment of political independence did not mean the end of economic exploitation and domination by imperialism. Although the single hegemony of British imperialism had been broken, a new form of integration was developed by the transnational corporate monopolies which moved in from the major imperialist states to compete in the newly opened fields of neo-colonialism. The policies put forward by the neo-colonial states, on the advice and encouragement of the three multilateral institutions, the World Bank, the I.M.F. and GATT, were designed to facilitate this new form of integration.

In agriculture, all production, whether on private farms in Kenya, on group farms and small peasant holdings in Uganda, or on the settlement villages *Ujamaa* villages in Tanzania, was for export to the monopolies in the imperialist states. East African villages were in effect integrated with the factories of Europe, the U.S. and Japan. The role of the state — whether small as in Kenya or large as in Tanzania — made no difference to the final outcome. The neo-colonial state was being used by the monopolies and a very small section of the comprador bourgeoisie who served their interests. The national bourgeoisie were dominated as a result and this reflected a dissatisfaction by the 'national' and petty bourgeoisies with imperialist exploitation which allowed them, weak as they were, hardly any room for self-expansion.

In manufacturing, the major theme that comes out of the analysis is the overwhelming power of transnational finance capital over import-substitution industry. Transnational finance capital challenged the hegemony of British finance capital, to make it merely one of the competing monopolies in the region. The reality of monopoly and competition among the various transnational monopolies, not only for agricultural products and industrial markets, but for the export of capital, became the very basis of petty competition within and between the territories, which vied to offer inducements to the different finance capitals on the 'best terms' possible for what was misguidedly regarded as 'national development'.

Such protection was the very thing desired by the transnational corporations, and provided the mechanism for concentrating and centralizing resources in East Africa in order to make super-profits for the monopolies. The individual national resources were thus made part and parcel of the total stock of finance capital at the disposal of transnational monopolies in realizing their global corporate objectives. And if the end result of the production process was the outflow of the surplus produced, as indeed it was, then there can be no doubt that the operations of the economies of the region were now under the law of concentration and centralization of capital on a global scale. The region's economies were just so many elements of the world resources open to the monopolies.

If development means more than a quantitative expansion of production, then these conditions make development impossible. Development on a national scale must imply the release of the productive forces from all fetters, the release of the full potential of a people and the enhancement of national pride and consciousness. It must include full political freedom for the downtrodden who produce the wealth and the realization of the fact that they can be in full control of their own destiny in transforming their society to a level that can uplift them from age-old backwardness and alien exploitation and domination. Development means the release of the enthusiasm of the people to undertake new tasks of a revolutionary character. This is the very basis for national development, for it is human beings who produce and develop themselves through their own activities.

Foreign control over resources in the present phase of vertical integration under conditions of neo-colonialism also means the creation of a class of local comprador agents. Incipient even in the early days of colonialism, this class was entrenched both by the 'Africanization' of commerce and other service industries, whether state-controlled or privately run, and by the privileges available from the large fees, discounts, commissions and graft meted out to them by the monopolies. The strengthening of these comprador forces can only frustrate efforts at national development since their economic interest lies in protecting and advancing the interests of the monopolies.

The new compradorial class in Kenya is reflected in the activities of the state, in the 'Africanization' of commerce and in land acquisitions by individuals. The pressure by the Kenyan petty bourgeoisie to reap the 'fruits of *Uhuru*' has become the very basis upon which international finance capital has established its agency for domination through the class structure in Kenya — the neo-colonial state and the comprador bourgeoisie. Since the major part of the productive sectors in land and industry, as well as in commerce, have always been controlled by monopolies, the weak Kenyan bourgeoisie and petty bourgeoisie has been only left side activities in trade, road transport, a bit of construction and petty manufacturing. In 1960, before Independence, out of the 19,000 or so licenced traders doing £260 million worth of business per annum, Kenyan African traders numbered only 1,400, handling £1 million worth of business a year.[1] As a result of measures taken by the neo-colonial state through the creation of two loan schemes —

the Joint Loans Board Scheme and financed through the Industrial and Commercial Development Corporation — designed to finance the takeover by Kenyan Africans from Asian traders, the traders found a niche in the channels of the international finance capital that bound them, in the words of Leys, 'tightly to the established foreign suppliers and to the state, making them into highly dependent clients, not entrepreneurs'.[2] 'The effect of this was to create a new stratum of the African petty bourgeoisie, ensconced within the general system of protection and monopoly, in such a way as to serve and complement foreign capital, not replace it.'[3]

This was also true in small manufacturing and construction, which was dependent on loans from the foreign-monopoly-dominated I.C.D.C., to purchase machinery, spares and, at times, raw materials from the same monopolies. Equally, on the land, the 'big man', who happened to be also in the trade and services sector appropriated the large farms with the help of loans from the state. Many of these 'big men' were ministers, M.P.s and senior civil servants who, because of their new economic position, began to identify themselves economically with their fellow large-scale European farmers.

This development should go a long way to disprove theories of a national bourgeoisie emerging in Kenya as a ruling class. Characteristic of neo-Trotskyist mystification, an otherwise well-researched book by Nicola Swainson,[4] which in fact proves the domination of finance capital over the Kenyan economy, claims to prove the opposite.

In Uganda state and private activities equally have led to a growth in the comprador class, which under Amin consolidated itself as the big *Mafuta Mingi*. This class must be analysed in the context of neo-colonial production relations and cannot be represented, as Mamdami tries to do, as the consolidation of the state 'governing bureaucracy' which failed to mature into a 'bureaucratic bourgeoisie'.[5] Indeed, it is only when the comprador class is separately identified, and its contradiction with the 'national' and petty bourgeoisie correctly grasped that we can comprehend the political crisis that led to the military coup in Uganda in 1971.[6]

In Tanzania, where the state took an active role in the economy, the compradorial class emerged in the very institutions that were supposed to fight the control of foreign capital over the economy. It was actually through the mechanisms of state participation that international finance capital was represented within the parastatal bodies set up to handle trade, insurance, banking and other financial institutions. In many cases, parastatals like the National Insurance Corporation — itself an agency for Lloyds International which underwrote its foreign commitments — worked very closely with private agents and brokers within Tanzania. In this way the state bodies generated business for private individuals — all acting as agents for international finance capital. The state officials whom Shivji saw fit to call a separate 'ruling class', i.e. the 'bureaucratic bourgeoisie',[7] were no more than the channel through which international monopolies and the local comprador class enhance their interests. Thus, the State Trading Corporation took over from 654 exclusive trade agencies, of which 223 were British, and itself became the main agency for importing goods from these monopolies.[8] This it did in close collaboration with the comprador bourgeoisie.

This period saw open bribery and corruption used by the monopolies as a means of competing for markets through state agencies. In this way the state officials were paid commissions to enhance their interest. Failure to specify this class concretely has led to a mistaken identification of the enemy by Shivji and by Mamdami with respect to Uganda and Tanzania, and Swainson with respect to Kenya.

In our view, a clear analysis of all class forces operating in the region, from the point of view of 'who are the people?' and '*who is the principal enemy now?*', would enable us to isolate a minute section of the comprador bourgeoisie and identify correctly the majority of the national forces that can be united to carry out the new national democratic revolution under the leadership of the proletariat. Politics in the three East African territories clearly show that, unless *the people as a whole* are mobilized in unity to advance the line of democracy and national independence, imperialist exploitation of the region will continue. Hence the need for ideological clarity, vigilance, unity and revolutionary action.

References

1. Colin Leys, *Underdevelopment in Kenya: The Political Economy of Neo-Colonialism* (London, Heinemann, 1975), p. 150.
2. *Ibid.*, p. 155.
3. *Ibid.*, p. 149.
4. Nicola Swainson, *The Development of Corporate Capitalism in Kenya* (London, Heinemann, 1980).
5. M. Mamdani, *Politics and Class Formation in Uganda* (London, Heinemann, 1975).
6. See D.W. Nabudere, *Imperialism and Revolution in Uganda* (London/ Dar es Salaam, Onyx Press/Tanzania Publishing House, 1979), Ch. 14.
7. I.G. Shivji, *Class Struggle in Tanzania* (London, Heineman, 1976).
8. M.Y. Yaffey, *Balance of Payments Problems of a Developing Country: Tanzania* (Munich, Welt-Forum, 1968), p. 26.

Other Books Available from Zed Press
On Africa

Robert Archer and Antoine Bouillon
The South African Game
Sport and Non-racialism in South Africa
Hb and Pb

Mohammed Babu
African Socialism or Socialist Africa?
Hb and Pb

Faarax M.J. Cawl
Ignorance is the Enemy of Love
(Trans. from Somali by Dr. G. Andrzejewski)
Pb

Basil Davidson
No Fist is Big Enough to Hide the Sky
The Liberation of Guinea and Cape Verde
Aspects of an African Revolution
Hb and Pb

Aquino de Braganca and Immanuel Wallerstein (eds.)
The African Liberation Reader
Documents of the National Liberation Movements of Southern Africa
Hb

Ronald Graham
Monopoly Capital and African Development
The Political Economy of the World Aluminium Industry
Hb

Edwin Madunagu
Problems of Socialism: The Nigerian Challenge
Pb

Elenga Mbuyinga
Pan Africanism or Neo-colonialism
The Bankruptcy of the OAU
Hb and Pb

Okwudiba Nnoli
Path to Nigerian Development
Pb

Christine Obbo
African Women
Their Struggle for Economic Independence
Hb and Pb

Pan African Handbook 1982
Pb

SWAPO Department of Information
To be Born a Nation
The Struggle for Namibia
Hb and Pb

A. Temu and B. Swai
Historians and Africanist History: A Critique
Hb and Pb

Ben Turok (ed.)
Development in Zambia
Hb and Pb

On Imperialism

Malcolm Caldwell
The Wealth of Some Nations
Hb and Pb

F. Clairmonte and J. Cavanagh
The World in Their Web
The Dynamics of Textile Multinationals
Hb

Ronald Graham
Monopoly Capital and African Development
The Political Economy of the World Aluminium Industry
Hb

Felix Greene
The Enemy
What Every American Should Know about Imperialism
Pb

Yan Fitt, Alexandre Faire and Jean-Pierre Vigier
The World Economic Crisis
American Imperialism at Bay
Hb and Pb

H.S. Marcussen and J.E. Torp
The Internationalization of Capital: The Prospects for the Third World
Hb

James F. Petras
Class, State and Power in the Third World
Hb

Zed Press titles cover Africa, Asia, Latin America and the Middle East, as well as general issues affecting the Third World's relations with the rest of the world. Our Series embrace: Imperialism, Women, Political Economy, History, Labour, Voices of Struggle, Human Rights and other areas pertinent to the Third World.

**You can order Zed titles direct from Zed Press,
57 Caledonian Road, London N1 9DN, U.K.**

DA